D0548680

	DATE DUE		

736
Jackson, Paul

GRAND COUNTY PUBLIC LIBRARY
25 South 1st East
Moab, UT 84532

ORIGAMI AND PAPERCRAFT

A STEP-BY-STEP GUIDE

ORIGAMI AND PAPERCRAFT

A STEP-BY-STEP GUIDE

GRAND COUNTY PUBLIC LIBRARY
25 SOUTH 1st EAST
MOAB, UTAH 84532

PAUL JACKSON AND VIVIEN FRANK

CRESCENT
BOOKS
NEW YORK

A QUINTET BOOK

This 1988 edition published by
Crescent Books, distributed by
Crown Publishers, Inc., 225 Park Avenue South
New York, New York 10003

Copyright © 1988 Quintet Publishing Limited.
All rights reserved. No part of this publication
may be reproduced, stored in a retrieval system
or transmitted in any form or by any means,
electronic, mechanical, photocopying,
recording or otherwise, without the permission
of the copyright holder.

LIBRARY OF CONGRESS
Library of Congress Cataloging-in-Publication
Data

Origami: a step-by-step guide.
p. cm.
ISBN 0-517-66804-1
1. Origami.
TT870. 066 1988
736' .982--dc19
88-10841
CIP

h g f e d c b a

This book was designed and produced by
Quintet Publishing Limited
6 Blundell Street
London N7 9BH

Art Director: Peter Bridgewater
Designer: Linda Henley
Editors: Sandy Shepherd, Judith Simons
Photographer: Andrew Sydenham
Stylists: Paul Jackson, Vivien Frank
Illustrator: Lorraine Harrison

Typeset in Great Britain by
Central Southern Typesetters, Eastbourne
Manufactured in Hong Kong by
Regent Publishing Services Limited
Printed in Hong Kong by
South Sea International Press Limited

ACKNOWLEDGEMENTS

The authors and publishers would like to thank the following companies for their generosity in supplying the materials used for the craftwork throughout this book: Compton Marbling, Falkiner Fine Papers, J Hewitt & Sons, Paperchase, Wiggins Teape Ltd, S F Williams (Foils) Ltd, Winsor & Newton. They would also like to thank the British Paper and Board Industry Federation for information, Jessica Dodd and Sue Matthews for invaluable assistance, Andrea Lyttleton for all calligraphy, Maureen Richardson for papermaking suggestions and June Tunmore for the paper flowers.

CONTENTS

Introduction 6

Paper and Equipment 7

Making Paper 15

Decorating Paper 31

Papier Mâché 51

Origami 57

Boxes and Bags 75

Wrapping Ideas 87

Twist-Outs, Cut-Aways and Pop-Ups 95

Stationery 103

Table Decorations 115

History of Paper 125

Index 126

INTRODUCTION

Paper is one of Man's greatest inventions. Think how many times a day you use it as writing paper, wallpaper, tissues, paper money, newspapers, books, magazines, envelopes, packaging, tickets, photographs, checks, computer printouts – the list is almost endless.

Think also of how many times a day you throw paper away. That list too is almost endless. The truth is that we do not always think about paper. We see it as a short-lasting, everyday material to be used and discarded. But think again!

For arts and crafts, paper is the most versatile of all materials. There are thousands of different papers in an enormous range of colors, weights and textures. Paper is readily available, usually inexpensive, simple to store and requires the help of only the most basic materials and equipment, such as scissors or glue, to transform it into any number of beautiful objects. Sometimes, as in origami, only the paper itself is used.

What is more, the variety of papercrafts is such that whether you like to make things that are decorative, practical, ingenious, geometric, or expressive, there is bound to be one craft that will appeal to you.

The projects inside have been chosen to show the diversity of papercrafts. They are divided loosely into two sections: the first shows how you can give a sheet of paper an interesting surface, either by making your own paper or by decorating existing sheets; the second introduces some three-dimensional papercrafts, such as napkin folding, papier mâché, pop-ups, boxes and bags, and paper flowers.

We, the authors, hope that our enthusiasm for all things paper will inspire you to make some of the projects, and that they will give you pleasure and satisfaction.

Paul Jackson

Vivien Frank

PAPER AND EQUIPMENT

Page 7 Top Crêpe and double crêpe papers are forms of tissue paper which have been passed through a patterned roller when wet; this gives them their characteristic crinkled and stretchy qualities.

Page 7 Bottom Textured papers. The texture is printed on and gives a soft looking, rich surface, although not as vibrant as patterned papers.

There are three types of paper: handmade, moldmade and machinemade and paper has two basic and important qualities – weight and grain. Handmade papers, which often incorporate long fibers, have no grain (the direction in which the fibers lie) and have four deckle edges (a deckle is the rough edge of the paper). Moldmade papers are less expensive than handmade ones and are made by machine, but have two deckle edges and longer fibers than those used in machinemade papers. Moldmade and machinemade papers both have a grain.

Other terms which are often used when talking about paper are "laid," "wove" and "sized." "Laid" paper is made on a mold which has wire, or sometimes wooden, bars laid across the frame. These bars allow a thinner deposit of pulp to be laid and leave an impression in the sheet of paper. This impression may be visible only against the light. Watermarks are formed in the same way. Paper without these lines is called "wove," from the woven mesh on which the pulp is poured. Paper can be "sized," which means that it is coated with a glue substance (usually gelatine or starch), or it can be "unsized." Sized paper is less absorbent than unsized and therefore ink or paint do not bleed when drawn or painted on it. Unsized paper is known as "waterleaf."

PAPER WEIGHT

Paper is usually measured by the weight in pounds of a ream (500 sheets) in its basic size. For example, the basic size of a sheet of bond paper is 17 × 22 inches. A ream of light bond paper in this size would weigh 16 pounds; thus, the paper is referred to as 16-pound bond. A ream of heavier bond paper would weigh 32 pounds and therefore be called 32-pound bond. Confusingly, different types of papers have different basic weights because the size of the sheet varies. Outside of the U.S. the metric system is used to define paper weights. In this system, the weight of the paper is independent of the size. Instead, the weight is expressed in grams per square meter (g/m^2).

Bottom left Decorated origami and gift-wrapping papers are printed as part of their manufacturing process. Some are printed on one side only, which increases their versatility in papercrafts.

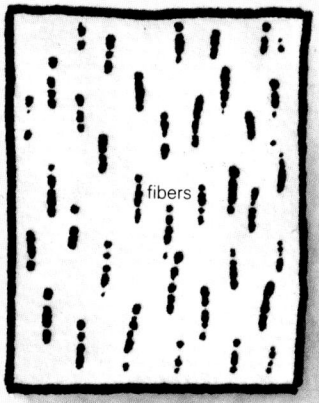

1 A sheet of paper with the grain running from top to bottom.

2 The sheet will bend easily when the lefthand edge is brought over to the right, because the bend follows the direction of the grain.

3 The sheet will not bend as easily when the top edge is brought down to the bottom, because the bend runs across the direction of the grain.

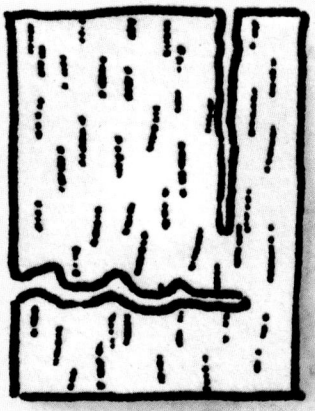

4 A torn edge is straighter when it follows the direction of the grain than when it runs across the grain.

PAPER GRAIN

The grain of paper is pronounced in machinemade papers because the mold on which they are made is a moving belt and the fibers settle in the direction of the movement of the belt. This grain can be used to advantage in that paper will fold, curve, tear and crease more easily along its grain. But it also has disadvantages: when wetted, as in gluing, the fibers swell widthways but not lengthways, and although they compress again when dry, if two surfaces are being joined, you may end up with a curved surface. To avoid this, try dampening both sheets of paper.

To find out which way the grain runs in a piece of paper, curl the paper in both directions and, while pressing gently with one hand, feel which way bends more easily. Another way, although somewhat extravagant, is to tear two strips from the paper, one in each direction. When you are tearing with the grain, the tear will be much cleaner and less irregular. There is also grain in card and board; discover this by flexing the sheet between your hands and then turning it through 90° and flexing it the other way; it will flex more readily in the direction of the grain.

Below Lightweight card (also called tag or oaktag) has many uses, from making templates to small boxes. Heavier card and corrugated paper can be used for packaging or surface decoration.

Right Foil papers are made by coating paper with adhesive and then with colored metal powders, which are then burnished. Embossing is often applied to metallic foils backed with paper, as here. This is done by running paper between rollers which have been engraved with a pattern.

Above Ingres (Strathmore) papers are often recognizable from their uneven surface appearance with visible hair-like fibers. They are lightweight to mediumweight papers.

Left Gift-wrap papers come in a huge range of patterns and textures and are printed onto white paper. The reverse is left unprinted. They are invaluable when decorative effects are needed.

Left Japanese papers are often extremely fine in appearance, but because they are made with long fibers, they are usually very strong.

Right Colored papers and card come in a wide range of weights and colors and are an attractive alternative or contrast to white.

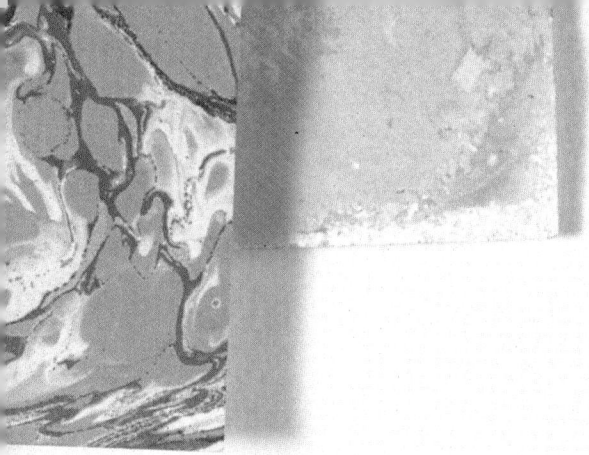

Above Marbled papers are formed by floating colored oil-based inks onto water. Paper is laid on top and then removed, pulling the inks with it. The best examples are marbled by hand, although cheaper printed sheets can also be purchased.

Below Handmade papers are the most beautiful of all papers. Their surfaces are rich in color and texture and will make any papercrafts project look extra special.

CRAFT EQUIPMENT

1 Felt-tipped pens
2 45° triangle
3 Small plastic ruler
4 M-shaped safety ruler
5 Metal cutting ruler
6 Mechanical pencil
7 Graphite (lead) pencils
8 Clear adhesive tape
9 Pencil sharpener
10 Glue stick
11 White glue
12 PVA adhesive
13 Round-tipped craft scissors
14 Retractable craft knife with snap-off blade
15 Double-sided adhesive tape
16 Scissors
17 Vinyl eraser
18 Self-healing cutting mat

MAKING PAPER

Left Here are just a few examples of the many effects of color, texture and design that guarantee making paper at home is such fun.

For most of its 2,000-year history, paper has been made by hand. However, since the Industrial Revolution in the late 18th century and the invention of machinery that could mass-produce paper, the craft has become a highly sophisticated industrial science. Yet making paper is essentially a simple process and one which is tremendous fun and surprisingly creative. It is a craft in which all the family can participate – even young children can make their own sheets of paper.

Traditionally, handmade paper is made from hemp or, more commonly, from recycled cotton rags. Both substances have unusually long fibers, which bind together well in the papermaking process to form a strong material. To make these fibers into paper they have to be broken down and separated, which means boiling them in caustic substances. To keep the method practical enough for you to try in your own kitchen, this chapter will deal only with recycling existing papers. Quite a few books have been written in recent years which explain how to make paper from plant fibers, so if you get the bug, look for them in your local library or bookshop.

SUITABLE PAPERS FOR RECYCLING

The best papers for making good white sheets include unprinted computer paper, typing paper, writing paper and photocopier paper. Other good, but more unusual, papers include Ingres (Strathmore) paper (all weights), drawing paper, watercolor paper, card, printed computer paper and old novels or picture books printed on good-quality paper. Even tissues, napkins and tea bags can be used. To help soften thicker papers and card, soak them overnight before blending them (see below).

Avoid using newspapers: they are made from cheap, poor-quality pulp which has a high acid content and turns brown very quickly. Also, avoid shiny papers such as glossy magazine paper: the coatings on these papers can turn into a sludge or a crumbly powder when recycled. Poster paper and other papers coated with a colored pigment should also not be used. If in doubt, always try out a paper. In truth, very few types are unsuitable for recyling.

MOLD-AND-DECKLE METHOD

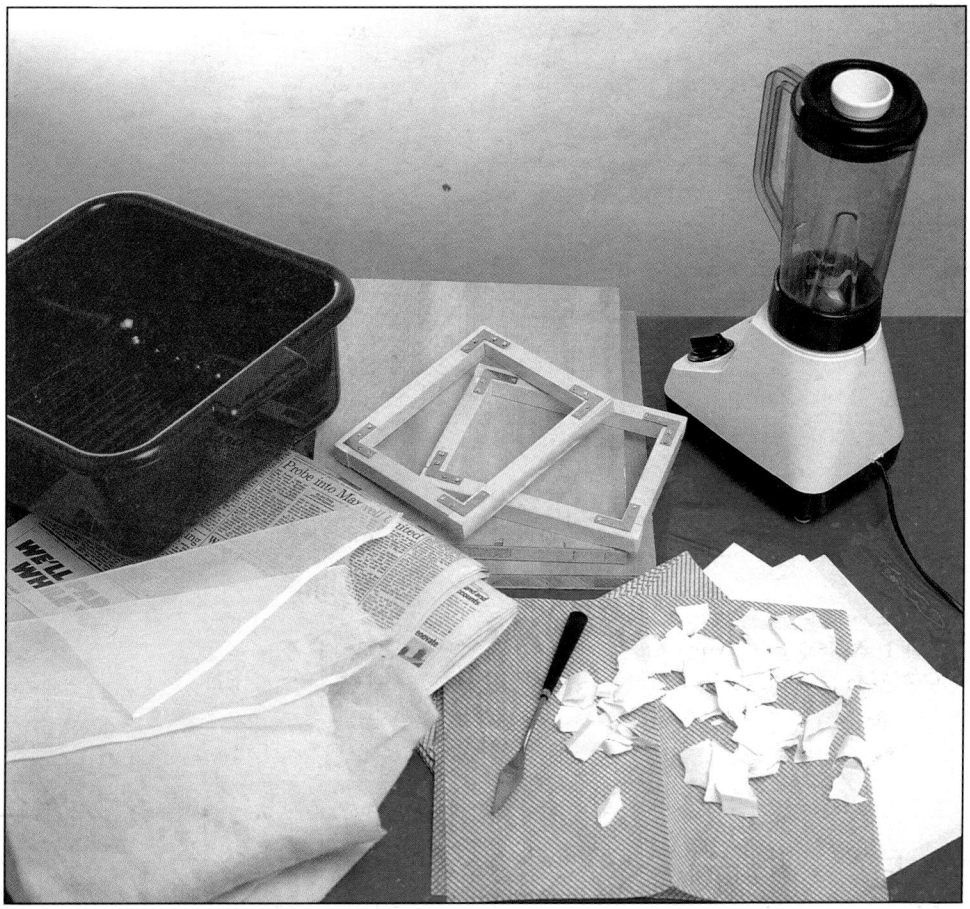

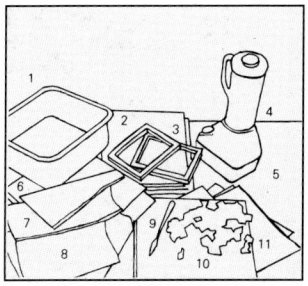

EQUIPMENT

1 Large oblong bowl or dishpan **2** Two wooden boards **3** Two wooden frames (see page 18) **4** Blender **5** Plastic sheeting **6** Large format newspapers **7** Curtain netting (see page 18) **8** Old bath towel **9** Palette knife **10** Kitchen cleaning cloths **11** Paper for recycling

This method makes thick sheets of paper because the deckle frame traps a lot of pulp on top of the mould. For thinner sheets, add extra water to the pulp.

EQUIPMENT

- Paper to be recycled.
- A blender. One with a 4 cup capacity container is the best, but any size will do. Paper is not poisonous, so rest assured that the container will not be contaminated.
- At least one large, oblong bowl or dishpan. Circular or oval ones are the wrong shape. Make sure they are very clean, or unwanted particles of dirt will appear in the paper pulp.
- An old bath towel to cut up, capillary matting (available from plant nurseries) or any other very absorbent material.
- Smooth, all-purpose, absorbent kitchen cleaning cloths (you will need one for each sheet of paper). Do not use coarse kitchen towels because they texture the paper when it is pressed, unless, of course, you want this texture.
- Plenty of clean newspaper, preferably broadside (large format), which has not been folded into quarters. If possible, start collecting well ahead of making paper because you will need a lot.
- Two sturdy wooden boards about 12 × 18 in. The boards need not be identical or clean, but the wood must be strong enough not to bend, so do not use Masonite or thin plywood.
- A palette knife.
- A few heavy books or other weighty objects.
- A large flat surface to work on.
- Plastic sheeting, trash bags or a waterproof tablecloth to cover the work surface and nearby carpets.
- A sink.

MAKING A MOLD AND DECKLE

You will need a mold and deckle on which to deposit the wet pulp before it is pressed and dried to become paper. They can be bought in craft shops or by mail from craft suppliers, but it is easy enough to make your own. If you have enough materials, it is well worth making a few sets of molds and deckles.

EQUIPMENT

- Enough ¾-in-square wood to cut four 8-in lengths and four 5-in lengths
- Plain curtain netting or similar open-weave fabric. The size of the mesh is not critical, but should not be too tight or too open
- Drawing pins (thumb tacks)
- Eight L-shaped brass plates (with screws), not wider than the wood
- A screwdriver

1 Cut the wood to the lengths described above, and arrange them to make two identical frames. Let the ends of the short lengths touch the sides of the long lengths. Screw the brass plates to the corners of one face only, to hold the frames together. Alternatively, if you have the equipment and necessary carpentry skills, miter the corners, apply a waterproof adhesive and nail them together.

2 Pin the curtain netting over the top face of one frame. A constant tension of net is important, so first pin it to the middle of one outside edge, then to the middle of the opposite outside edge, pulling it reasonably tight. Pin the middles of the two remaining outside edges, then begin to work toward the corners, pulling the net reasonably tight and pinning it as you go.

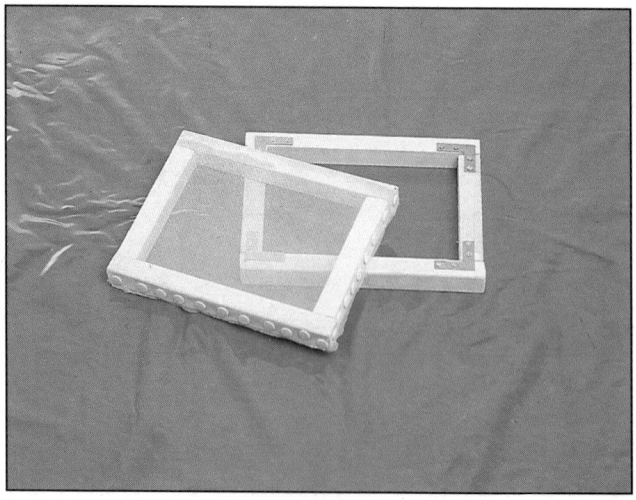

3 To complete, fold over the net at the corners to make a neat finish. Trim off the excess net. This frame is the mold, and the uncovered one the deckle. The mold and deckle can be made much larger, but you will not be able to use them in a bowl. A baby bath is a good alternative.

PREPARING THE PULP

The pulp can be prepared in advance and can be done by young children who greatly enjoy ripping paper to shreds! Tear several layers of paper at once to speed the process.

1 Tear (never cut) the paper to be recycled into pieces about the size of large postage stamps. Fill the blender no more than three-quarters full of water and put in no more than 35 torn pieces of paper for every 4 cups of water. Turn the blender on.

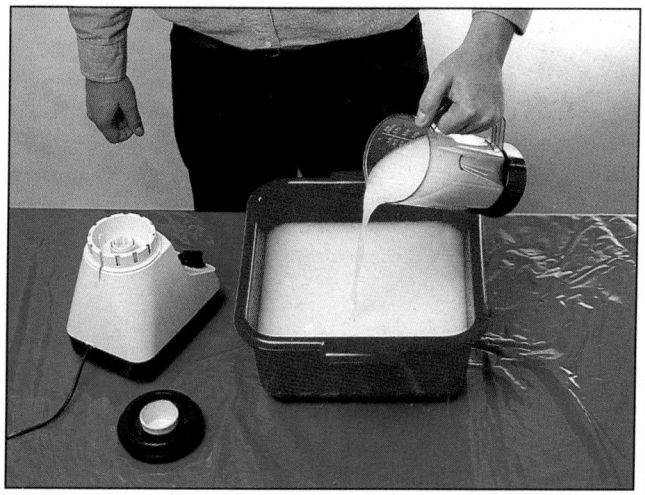

2 Pour the pulp into the bowl. Repeat the blending process until the bowl is half to two-thirds full, but not brimming over.

BLENDING TIMES

As a rough guide, blend computer, photocopy, typing, writing and similar papers for 25–35 seconds, drawing paper and Ingres (Strathmore) papers for 40–50 seconds, tissue for 60 seconds and card for 70–90 seconds (less if previously soaked overnight in water). The result should be a thin fibrous soup. If globules of fiber are still coagulating, blend for a little longer. If the machine is overheating, take out some of the paper. Do not be tempted to overload the container.

FORMING THE SHEET

Stir the pulp gently with your hand to distribute the fibers evenly in the water. Unstirred, they soon settle to the bottom. Repeat this every time the pulp is left to stand for more than a few minutes. This agitation is an important part of the process: be careful not to forget it as it will affect the success of this project.

1 Fit the deckle exactly over the mold, so that the brass plates on the deckle are on the top surface away from the mold, and the net on the mold rests against the deckle in the middle of the "sandwich."

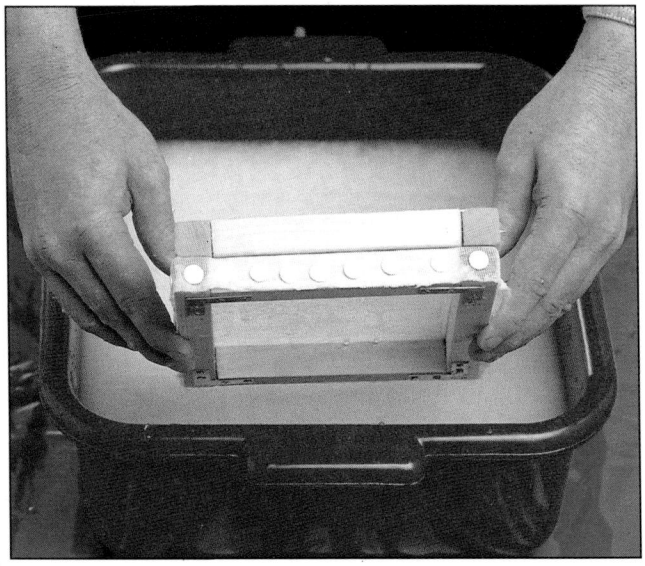

2 Hold the long edges of the mold and deckle together tightly at the far end of the bowl, making sure that the deckle is facing you.

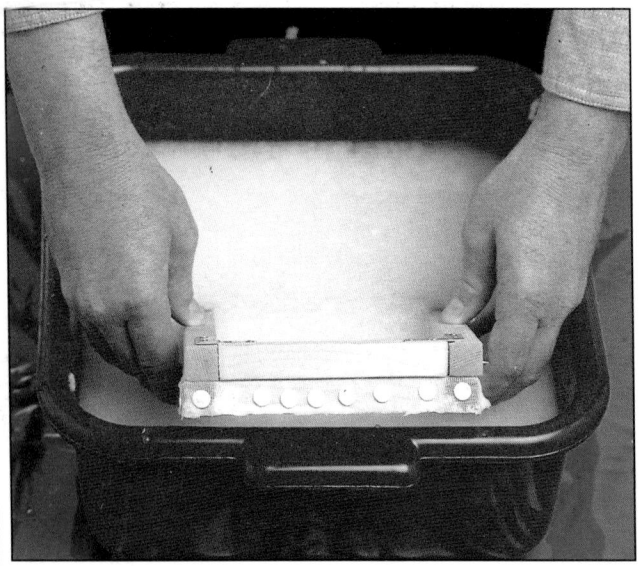

3 Then, with smooth movements, lower the short edges of the mold and deckle vertically into the pulp.

4 Pull the mold and deckle toward you while at the same time bringing them to a horizontal position under the pulp, with the deckle on top of the mold.

5 Lift the mold and deckle straight out of the pulp, being careful to keep them horizontal. Hold them a few inches above the pulp and let the excess water drain through, at the same time shaking them gently backward and forward, left and right, to help the fibers settle evenly on the net as the water drains.

6 Rest two adjacent edges of the mold on the nearside corner of the bowl.

7 Support the underside of the mold with one hand, and with the other, lift off the deckle quickly. Be careful not to drag the deckle into the pulp on the net, or it will damage the edge of the paper. Also avoid letting water drip off the deckle onto the pulp.

8 The pulp is now ready for couching.

COUCHING

This is a traditional term for transferring wet pulp from the mold onto the sheet of material on which it will dry. Before forming the sheet of wet pulp on the mold, prepare a couching mound. Make this from an old bath towel which has been cut up, capillary matting, or any other very absorbent material.

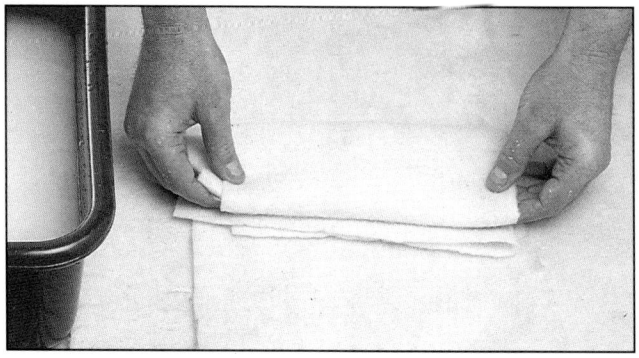

1 Cut up the material to make a small mound the same shape and size as the mold. Wet it to help it lie flat. (Take some time to do this properly.)

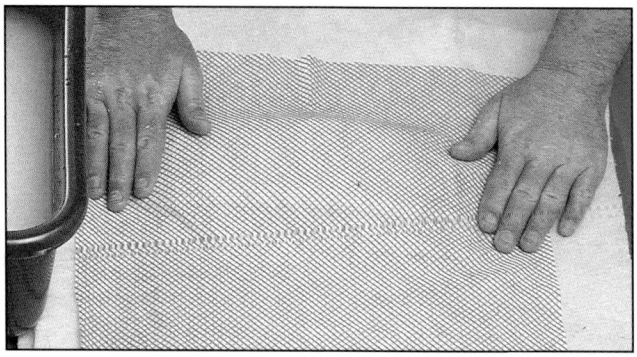

2 Cover the mound with a damp, all-purpose kitchen cleaning cloth, so that the nearside short edge of the cloth just covers the nearside edge of the mound.

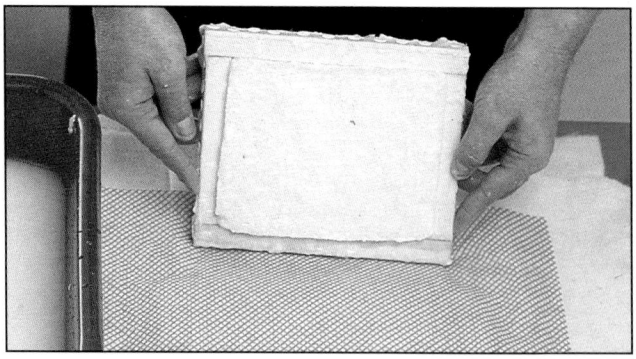

3 To form the wet pulp on the mound, rest the long edge of the mold on the cloth 1 in in front of the foot of the mound, so that the pulp is on the far side of the mold, facing the mound. Hold as shown.

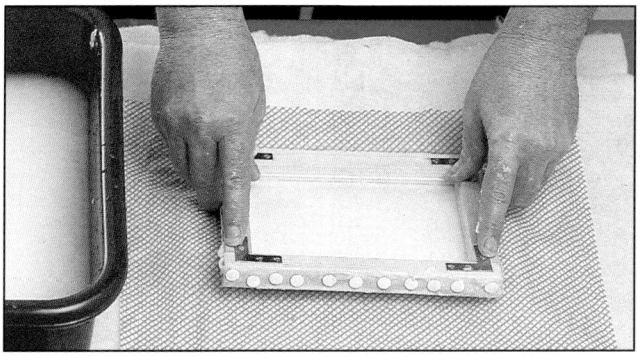

4 In as fluent a movement as possible, lower the sides of the mold gradually onto the mound, pressing firmly.

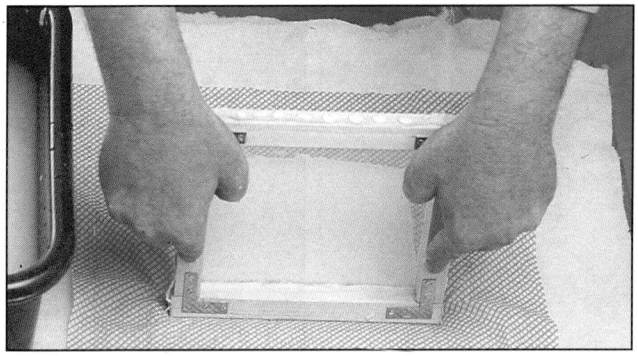

5 Lift the bottom edge off the cloth, pushing the top edge firmly into the cloth.

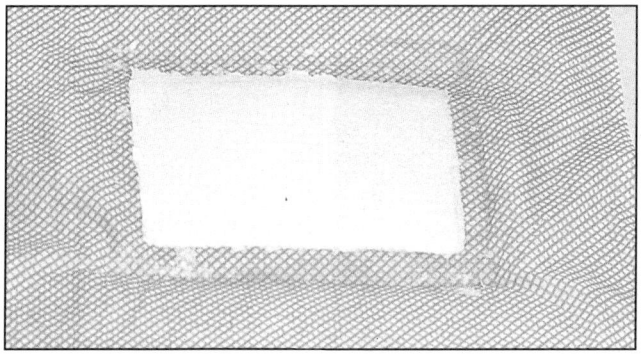

6 The pulp should stick to the cloth. If it doesn't, this is probably because the mound is too tall, too flat or has the wrong dimensions. Experiment with its shape until the pulp couches satisfactorily. Alternatively, the cloth may be too dry; wet it again.

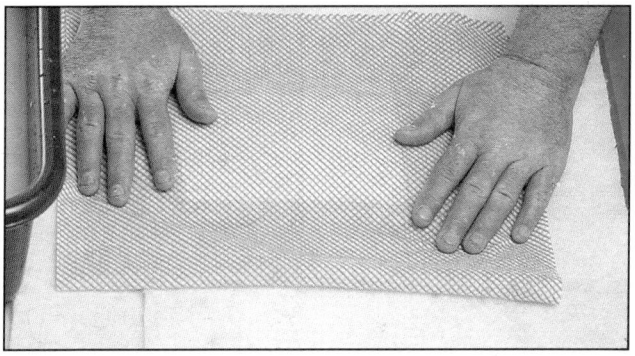

7 Fold the remainder of the cloth over the sheet of pulp. Be very careful not to leave any creases in the cloth where it covers the pulp, or they will be molded into the sheet when it is pressed, spoiling its smooth surface.

8 Lay a second damp cloth over the first and couch another sheet onto it as described above. Fold the cloth in half as before.

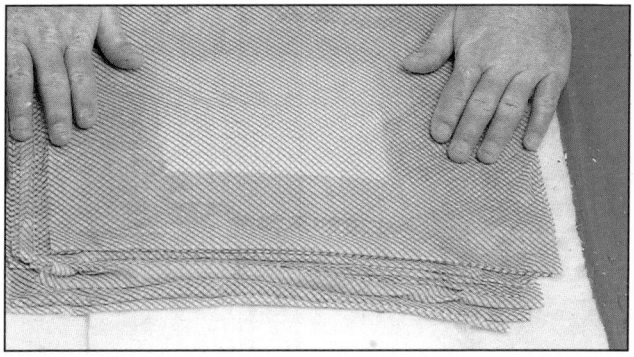

9 The process can be repeated a dozen times or more, each new sheet being couched on top of the others in a growing pile. Do not forget to lay out a new damp cloth for every sheet so that each is in its own folded cloth "sandwich."

PRESSING

The method described here looks very rough and ready (it is!), but works extremely well. A more professional way would be to use a real paper press. They are, however, quite expensive and difficult to find.

1 Put the pile of couched sheets onto one half of the back page of a broadside (large format) newspaper. Fold the other half of the newspaper over the pile, sandwiching the sheets in the middle.

2 Put the sandwich between two sturdy wooden boards.

3 Stand on the boards for about two minutes, squeezing out most of the water from the cloths. The heavier you are the better. This is best done out of doors, because a surprising amount of water will come out. Alternatively, do it on a bathroom floor or other tiled floor which can be mopped dry.

CAUTION!!

Unless you have a waste-disposal unit, when you empty the bowl of pulp at the end of a paper-making session, do not pour it down a sink. The fibers will congeal in the sump, causing a blockage. Instead, drain the pulp through a strainer so that the water drains into the sink. Put the dough-like pulp that has remained in the strainer into the trash, or use it to make a deckle-only sheet of paper (see page 26).

DRYING

This is the stage which is easiest to rush, but you must be patient. Let the paper dry at its own pace. Attempts to speed the process by ironing the paper or placing it near a heater may "cockle" (warp) it.

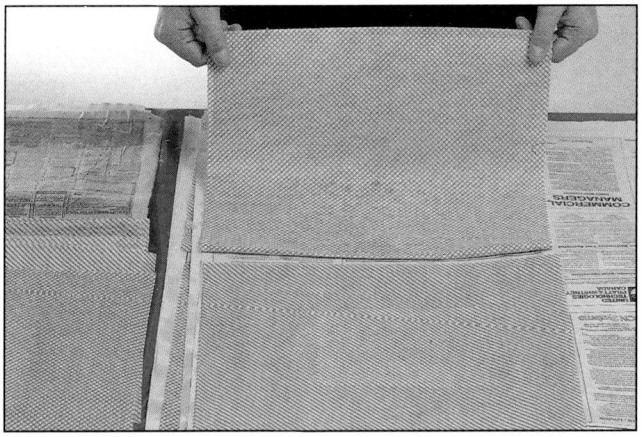

1 Remove the pile of damp cloths from the sodden newspaper. Take a new, dry newspaper and turn over three sheets to pages six and seven. Lay out two cloths on page six, then turn over three more sheets, covering the cloths, and lay out two more cloths on page twelve. Repeat the process until the newspaper is full. Turn to the back page and fold the newspaper in half from top to bottom across the middle. Repeat with other newspapers until all the cloths have been laid into them.

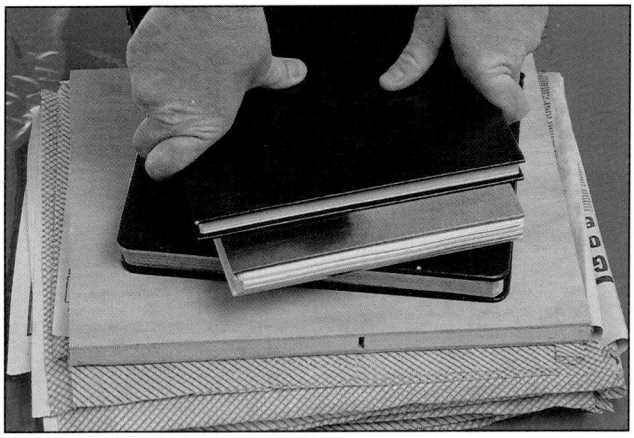

2 Put the newspapers back between the boards and weight them with a few large books or other objects of a similar weight. After about two hours, remove the cloths from the newspapers and lay them out as before into fresh newspapers. Once again weight them between the boards and leave for a few hours. Repeat the laying-out process every six hours or so until the cloths and the handmade paper are completely dry. This may take a day or more, depending on how thick the paper is and how much water it held originally.

3 When the paper is completely dry, open the cloths and gently slip a palette knife under the edge of the paper. Move it slowly under the sheet all round in a sequence of slicing movements, separating the paper delicately from the cloth. It is possible to do this with an ordinary kitchen knife, but a palette knife is easier to use and kinder to the paper, particularly if it is thin.

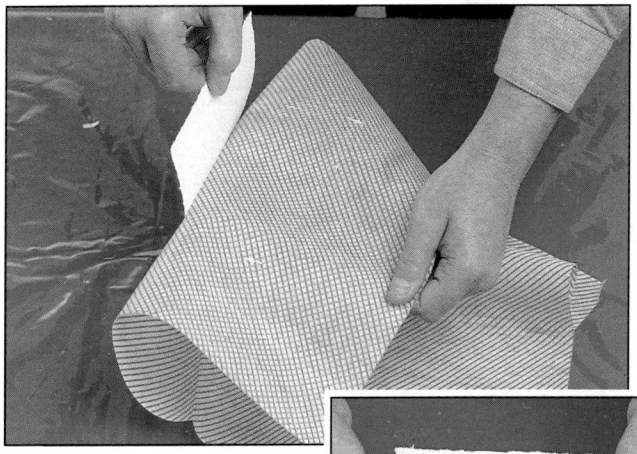

4 Hold an edge of the paper and peel off the cloth. Do not hold the cloth and pull the paper off because this will bend the paper and possibly damage it. The paper is now finished (**right**).

OTHER METHODS

THE MOLD-ONLY METHOD

The mold-and-deckle method but without the deckle will produce a thinner sheet because the absence of a deckle means that less pulp is held on the mold.

Use the mold without the deckle to produce finer sheets. If the pulp is already watery, the sheets formed using this process will be extremely thin and beautifully delicate.

SIZING

This process is necessary to stop inks and paints from bleeding into paper when they are written or drawn on. Unsized paper acts like blotting paper, diffusing a line of color, though this can sometimes be an attractive effect.

To size a sheet, simply add two teaspoons of laundry starch to the bowl of pulp. Stir it and continue making the paper as before. If you want a smooth writing surface, press the sheets with a medium-cool iron when they are nearly dry. Never iron the paper directly, but do it through a layer of fabric.

THE DECKLE-ONLY METHOD

This is a rough-and-ready method for making paper, or at least a fibrous mat, without the need for a net stretched over the deckle.

1 Blend the pulp for about one-third longer than the usual time, then pour it through a strainer. The water will drain away to leave a thick dough-like pulp trapped in the strainer.

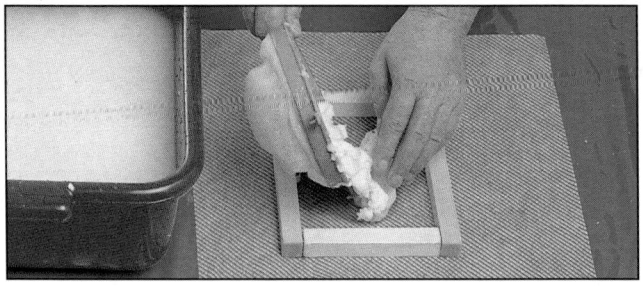

2 Lay out a damp kitchen cloth and place a deckle onto one half of it. Empty the contents of the strainer into the frame and spread it about evenly to make a pulp mat. Strain as much pulp as is needed to form a mat ¼-½ inch thick. If you have a pipette or turkey baster on hand, squirt some thin pulp onto the mat to help it bind.

3 Remove the deckle and fold the remainder of the cloth over the pulp. Press and dry as described for the mold-and-deckle method.

CREATIVE EFFECTS

SPECKLED SHEETS

You may think, and with reason, that it is a little odd to tear up a piece of paper, only to reconstitute it so that it looks pretty much the same at the end as it did at the beginning!

If these are your thoughts, look at the following creative suggestions. It is at this point that papermaking becomes an open-ended art form, where the only limitation is your imagination. Assume no rules, no right or wrong, just enjoy it. You will be surprised how often a silly idea, or indeed a silly mistake, can give a beautiful result.

1 Make a bowl of white pulp. Blend a small quantity of orange paper in a little water for about 10 seconds, so that it is not quite pulped, but shredded into small speckled pieces, and pour it into the white pulp.

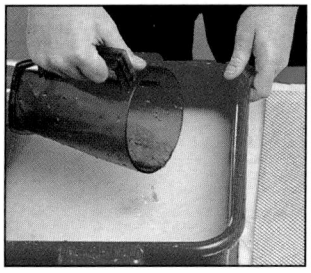

2 Repeat the previous step with a similar quantity of gray paper.

3 Form the sheet on the mold as before (with or without a deckle), then couch, press and dry. The sheet will be white with orange and gray speckles.

Above Try speckling the paper with white speckles in a colored pulp, or with any other combination of colors. As an alternative, blend tea leaves in a little water and add them to a white or colored pulp. You could also add small objects directly to the pulp without blending them: seeds, short lengths of hair or colored threads, confetti, small scraps of fabric, colorful flower petals or autumn leaves, all make an attractive effect when embedded in the paper.

LAID-ON EFFECTS

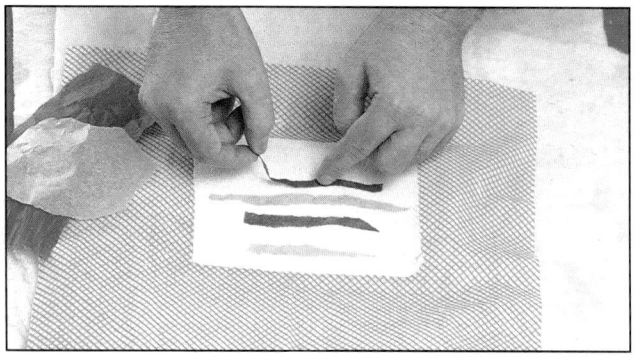

1 Couch a white sheet. Then tear up strips or cut out shapes from sheets of colored tissue paper and lay them on top of the couched sheet. As the sheet dries, the tissue will remain stuck to it.

2 To achieve subtle colored effects try the following method. Couch a sheet and lay tissue paper, thicker paper, wool or whatever you choose on top. Form another sheet using the mold only and couch it exactly over the top of the first sheet. This traps the colored items between two layers of pulp, but they will still be visible, if only faintly.

TIPS

- Try creating laid-on effects with thin and thick pieces of colored paper. With thick pieces, press and dry the paper on the couched sheets, then peel it off. Some of its colored pigment will have run off onto the main sheet to form a colored shadow (see left).
- Other interesting laid-on effects can be created with tickets, wool, petals, leaves (see left), sand, etc.

SHAPED PULPS

1 Couch a white sheet and mix a bowl of colored pulp. Hold an edge of the mold (without the deckle) and drag part of it vertically through the pulp, net side first.

2 Remove the mold from the pulp – the pulp will be deposited onto only part of the mold. Couch it over the top of the white sheet.

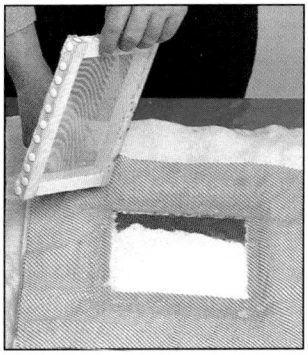

3 The colored pulp will cover part of the white pulp. Press and dry as before. Various effects can be achieved (**below**).

TIPS

- Try mixing up a few different colored pulps and couching them on the same sheet, or dragging a corner of the mold through the pulp, in order to change the shape of the pulp on the mold.
- To achieve more complex shapes of colored pulp, stick a paper shape to the top of the net, leaving holes where the pulp has to couch. Put all the mold under the pulp in the conventional manner. Pull it out and remove the paper shape, taking part of the pulp with it. Those parts of the net that were not covered with the paper will have retained pulp. Couch onto a previously couched sheet.

USES FOR HANDMADE PAPERS

Plain white sheets or sheets of a pale color make very attractive writing paper. For thin writing paper, form the sheets on a mold without a deckle, see page 26. If you do not want the writing inks to run, remember to size the pulp, see page 26. Thicker sheets make unusual business cards, calling cards, gift tags or place cards. To form the small shapes needed for business cards, either make a very small mold and deckle, see page 18, or mask part of a larger mold with a paper shape, see page 29.

Left To make greeting cards, glue a sheet of your paper to the front of an ordinary piece of card which has already been folded down the middle. Another sheet of handmade paper, possibly plain and starched, can be glued inside the card to hold a written greeting. Perhaps the most effective use of creative papers is to assemble a patchwork of sheets and frame them. Sheets which may be considered not good enough to become greeting cards, or which are too eccentric, become surprisingly attractive as a patchwork. Framed, they are always a talking point.

DECORATING PAPER

There is an infinite number of ways to decorate paper, some of which will be explained in this chapter. Within each method there are many variations, because the results will differ depending on the type and color of paper used. For example, ink on tissue paper will give a very strong color, but if you thin the ink and splatter it on a heavy, absorbent, colored paper the effect will be much more subtle.

Some of the techniques discussed will produce finished work, and others are only a step toward a bigger project. Just the basics of each method have been explained, but we hope your imagination will be stimulated to experiment and take them further.

WEAVING

EQUIPMENT

- Various mediumweight papers
- Adhesive tape
- Glue stick
- Scissors or craft knife
- Metal ruler
- Pencil

Paper weaving can be extremely challenging but can also be very simple. It can be used in a purely decorative way to make a picture or in a more practical way to form a box. The pleasure comes in the many exciting types and colors of paper you choose to use for your efforts. The main thing to remember is that there are no rules and the experimenting is all part of the fun. The paper used can be colored, patterned or textured, or even illustrations from magazines.

1 Using a metal ruler and a craft knife, cut strips of paper. These will provide straight edges in the pattern. Use a variety of colors, if desired.

2 Alternatively, tear strips to create a looser-edged pattern. Use different colors for greater effect.

3 When you are combining strips of paper in a woven design, the vertical strips represent the "warp" threads and the horizontal strips the "weft" threads, as in any form of weaving. Cut the warp into zigzags and thread different colored and textured strips through it.

4 Alternatively, cut the warp into curves for a wavy pattern and thread different colored weft strips through it.

5 For a more random effect, tear the strips and lay them across and through each other. The warp can be spread out and the weft can be woven irregularly so that spaces show between the strips.

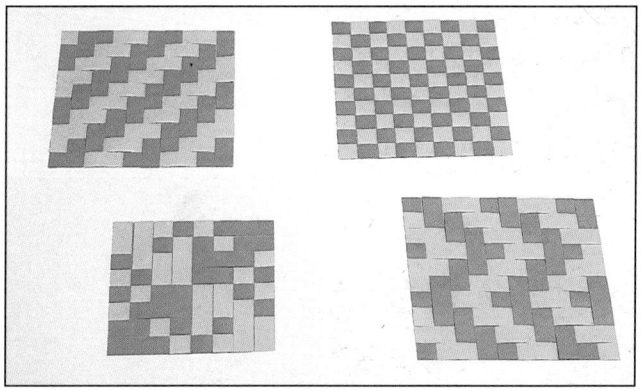

Above Rigid, geometric patterns are produced with straight-edged strips.

Right Create interesting patterns with irregular warp and weft strips.

COLLAGE

EQUIPMENT

- Lightweight to mediumweight paper
- Colored tissue paper
- Japanese papers
- Glue stick
- Gummed papers
- Foil papers
- Decorated adhesive tape
- Self-adhesive stickers

TIPS

- Although expensive, decorative Japanese papers can also be used to great effect.
- If time is short or you do not feel very creative, make decorative patterns by covering plain papers with bought stickers or sticky patterned tapes, or with your own shapes cut out from pregummed papers.

The word collage comes from the French verb *coller,* meaning "to stick." Collage is regarded as an art form and the examples shown here can be developed further.

1 Tear up small pieces of tissue paper and place on glued lightweight paper, using a glue stick.

2 Leave some edges of the tissue paper unattached and allow them to overlap a little. Finished sheets can be cut up and used on the front of a greeting card, see pages 104 and 105.

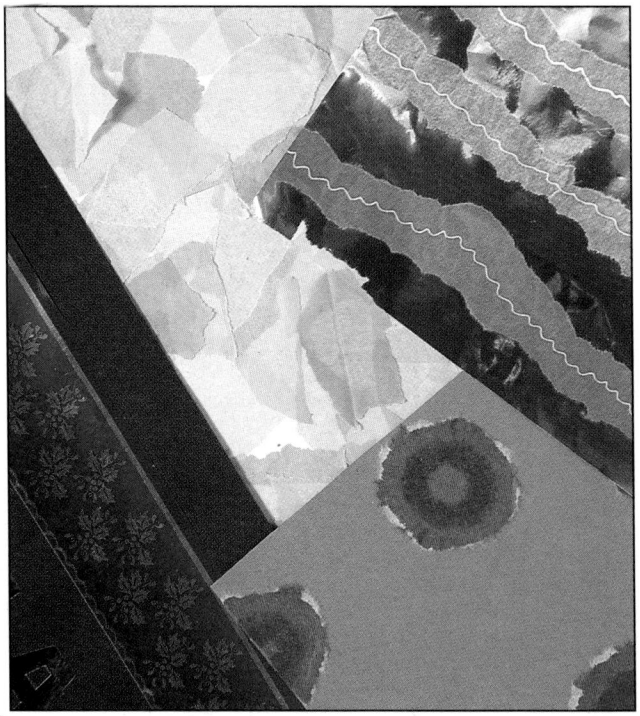

Above These finished examples can be used for many of the projects covered later in the book.

CAUTION!!

Remember that the dyes used in tissue paper are not usually colorfast, so take this into account when you are using different colors: yellow and purple may look nice next to each other, but mixed together the result will be a murky brown!!

STENCILING

EQUIPMENT

- Mediumweight paper
- Stencil paper
- Self-adhesive shapes
- Foil
- Plant mister
- Toothbrush
- Stencil brush
- Sponge
- Paint brush
- Paints and paint palette
- Colored inks, felt-tipped pens and colored pencils

Stenciling can be messy, so it is advisable to protect the working area and surrounding surfaces with newspaper to avoid accidents. The patterns in this section are mostly created by blocking out an area of paper and coloring the remaining part. The blocking out can be done using several kinds of stencils.

Above Cut shapes out from stencil paper. Both the negative and positive parts of the stencil can be used.

Left and below Fold a sheet of paper and cut or tear shapes out of the folded edges. Color through or round the shapes onto another piece of paper.

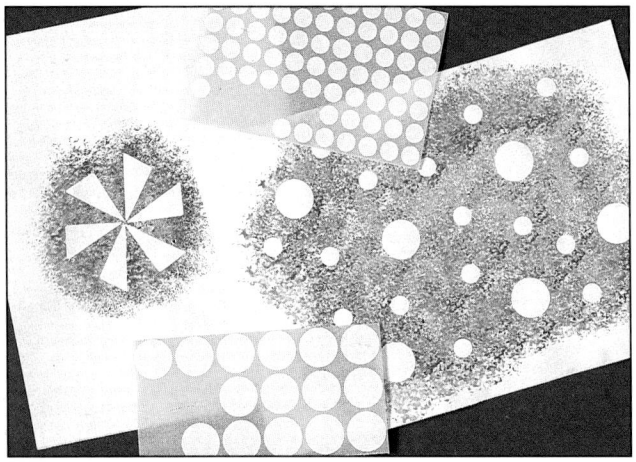

Try using self-adhesive shapes as stencils. Paint over them and then remove when dry.

Cut shapes out of a folded sheet of foil. Unfold the shape and brush one color through it. Swivel the stencil round slightly and paint through it with another color to create an attractive kaleidoscopic effect.

You can apply color in a number of ways. Try brushing the color on with an ordinary paint brush, or for a more stippled texture, use a stencil brush.

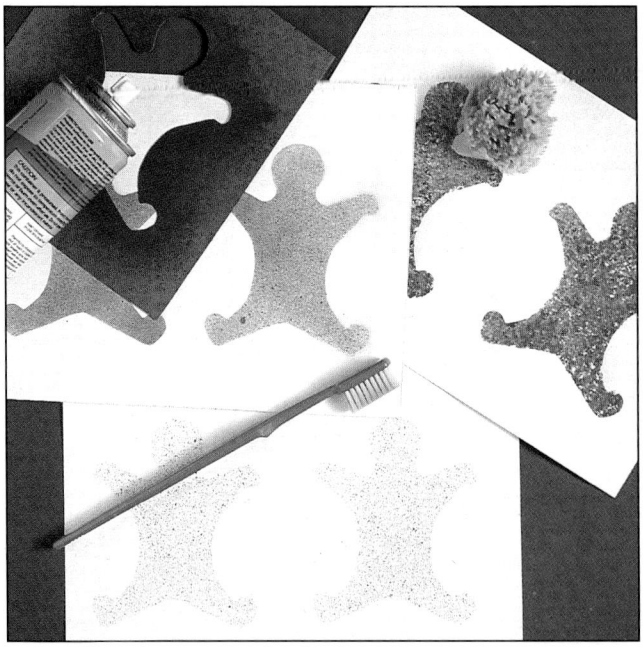

If you apply the color with a sponge, some of the cellular texture of the sponge will transfer onto the paper. For an even effect, use a spray can or airbrush. For a fine stippled effect, splatter the paint onto the paper from a toothbrush or a larger brush. Dip the brush in the liquid paint and shake off the excess before drawing a finger or ruler across the bristles. Keep the bristles facing downward!

1 Using a leaf-shaped positive stencil, paint is applied to a colored background with a sponge.

2 Using the cut-out leaf shape as a negative stencil, paint around the shape with a stencil brush.

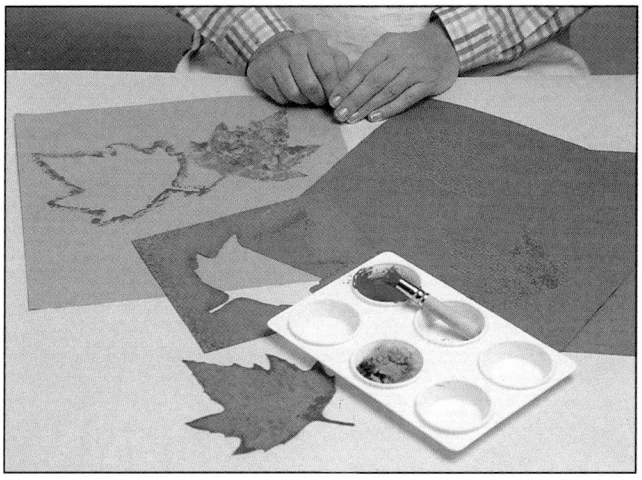

3 You can have great fun experimenting with these methods. Try using several colors in one design, or use colored paper as the background as this will add to the design.

STENCILING TIPS

- Spray the paper with water first before you stencil onto it, to increase its absorbency; the colors will spread more when you apply the paint.
- Do not make the paint too wet or it will run under the edge of the stencil.
- Do not load too much coloring medium on the brush or sponge, or the texture of the mark will be lost.
- Folded paper stencils cannot be used too often because they absorb the paint and become too sodden to be used cleanly.
- When using self-adhesive shapes, allow them to dry before you remove them to make sure that you do not smudge any part of the design.
- Try using acetate as a stencil material, and cut it with a scalpel or craft knife. As it does not tear, this material allows for quite a lot of detail and also has the advantage of being transparent so it can be positioned exactly with ease.
- Try tearing a large shape from a piece of paper and place it on another sheet; paint over the edges all around the shape. Lift off and tear off the painted edge, making the shape smaller and changing it slightly. Reposition it within the painted area and, perhaps with another color, paint over the new edge. Repeat the same process as many times as possible.

Above Here are just a few of the many varied effects that can be created using the stenciling techniques described in this section.

RESIST METHODS

EQUIPMENT

- Wax crayons
- Wallpaper paste
- Wax candles
- Poster (alkyd) paints
- Bowl
- Wide brush
- Black drawing ink
- Mediumweight to heavyweight paper

These methods can be tightly controlled or very random. They can be done with wax crayons and paint, wax rubbings and paint, paste and paint, or wax crayons and ink. Wax crayons and paint and wax rubbings and paint are very similar in application, although the final result is very different in that the first can be used to create a picture, whereas the second produces a pattern. Paste and paint is not strictly a resist method, but the end result looks similar to other resist methods. It is a good way of making textured patterns on paper.

WAX RUBBINGS AND PAINT

1 Cover a textured surface, such as a strip of plastic netting, with a piece of white or colored mediumweight paper and rub a candle or colored wax crayon over the paper. Remove it from the textured surface.

2 Next, brush some thin water-based paint over the entire sheet. The paint can be one color or can be brushed on in stripes of different colors.

3 Make sure that you brush the paint right over the edges of the paper, and protect the surrounding area with scrap paper. Allow the paper to dry naturally.

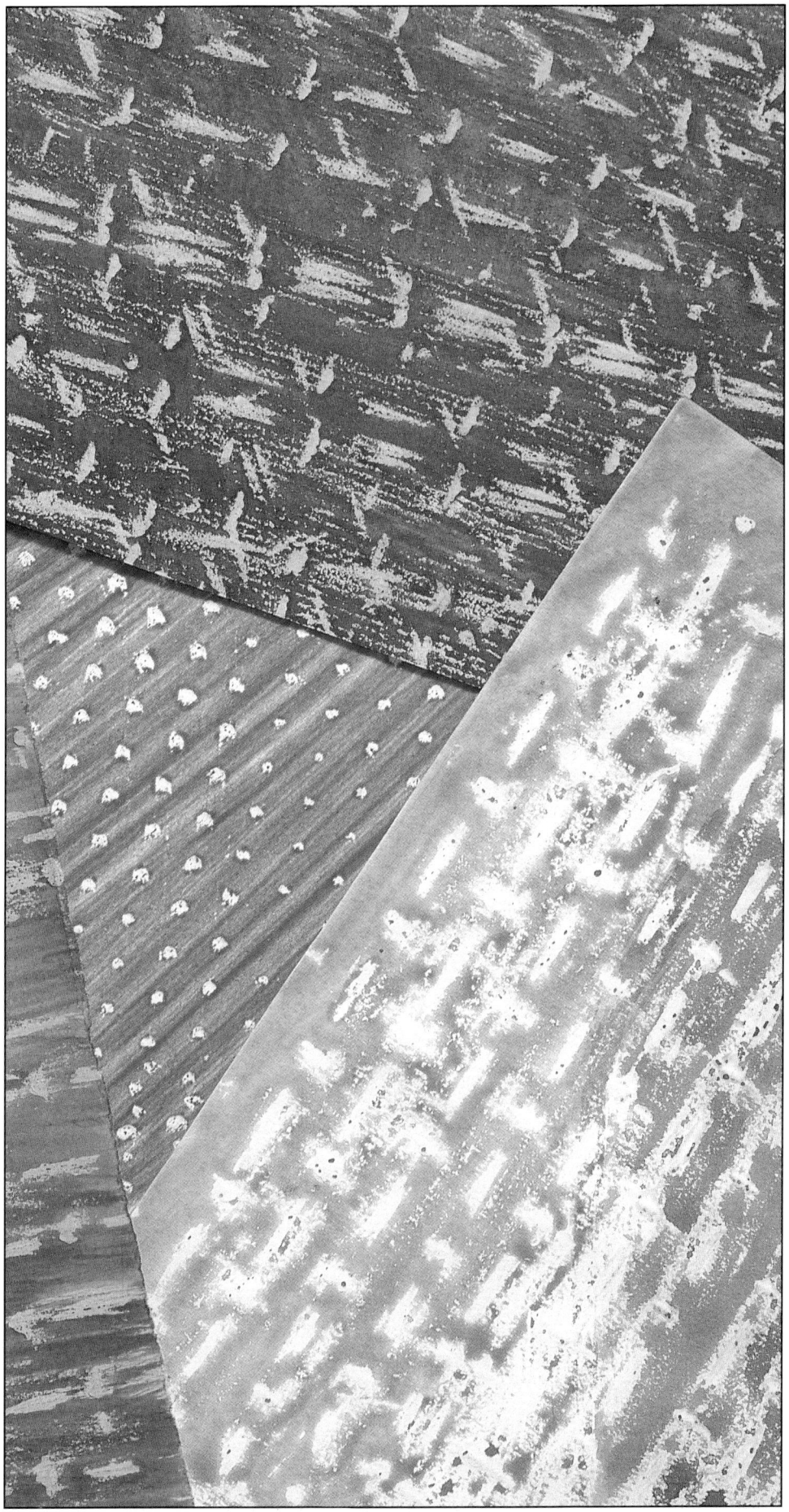

TIPS

- Mix the paint wash thinly and always mix enough to cover the whole sheet, ensuring an even tone of color.
- Use a wide brush to cover large areas: this will save you time and effort.
- It is possible to use thin paper for this method. If you mount it onto another sheet of lightweight paper it will be strong enough to make a box or bag, see pages 76–86.

Left These examples show a variety of rubbings on papers of different textures. Look around you for different materials which can be used for rubbings: cane chair seats, tennis rackets, brick walls, tree bark – the list is endless.

PASTE AND PAINT

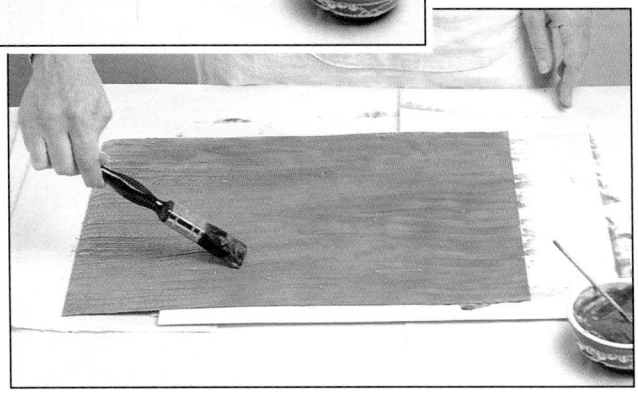

1 Mix wallpaper paste using the directions on the box – it should be reasonably thick but not lumpy. Add water-based paint to this mixture. Test the intensity of the color on a piece of paper (**top**). Using a broad brush, spread the paste mixture across the whole sheet as evenly as possible (**above**).

2 Now let your imagination take over. Using a finger, the handle of a paint brush or an improvised comb (as above), draw patterns in the paste and paint mixture.

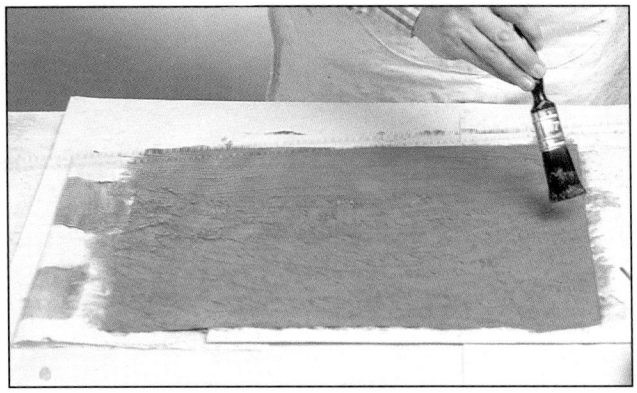

3 If you do not like the design, simply brush over it and start again! Depending on the amount of paste you use, the patterned paper will take quite a while to dry. To create a lighter appearance, when the paper is almost dry, lay a piece of thin paper (newsprint or similar) on top of the pasted paper and rub evenly over it, or use a roller, and then peel it off.

Right An infinite range of attractive designs can be created using different implements to pattern the paste mixture.

WAX CRAYONS AND INK

1 Using the crayons, draw bands or areas of color on to heavyweight paper. If you would prefer a black and white design, use white candle wax on white paper. Now, paint over the entire area with black drawing ink. It may be necessary to repeat this step in order to cover the wax crayon completely.

2 When the ink is dry, take any improvised drawing tool – the handle of a paint brush, the bottom of a pencil (**above**), an empty ballpoin pen, or the end of a ruler (**top**) – and scratch through the ink to reveal the colors of the crayons. Either draw a picture or make a pattern; whichever you choose the results will be stunning.

TIP

The above process can be reversed – paint an area with black paint, and when it is dry, color in areas over it with the wax crayons, pressing firmly onto the paint. Then scratch through the wax areas to reveal black lines or shapes, giving more detail to the crayoned design. This method creates a more individual design than the wax band of color painted with ink.

Left The two finished examples here show both random and controlled techniques.

DIPPING AND FOLDING

EQUIPMENT

- Thin absorbent paper
- Paper towels
- Small dishes
- Colored ink, food coloring or watercolor paint
- Stiff brush
- Bulldog clips
- Roller

This method is simple, quick, colorful and, for these reasons, very exciting. It involves folding paper in various ways and then dipping it into a colored liquid.

It is essential that you use very lightweight paper for this process, but you will have to experiment with different brands to discover which papers work best. For the photographed examples here, colored tissue papers and large sheets of lens tissue, available in some specialist paper shops, have been used. Many of the tissue papers sold in packets are not colorfast, and when they are wet their color may run. This can add to the design, but you should be aware of this possibility. It may be advisable to wear surgical rubber gloves while working with your chosen coloring medium (household gloves are too cumbersome to enable you to unfold the wet tissue without tearing it).

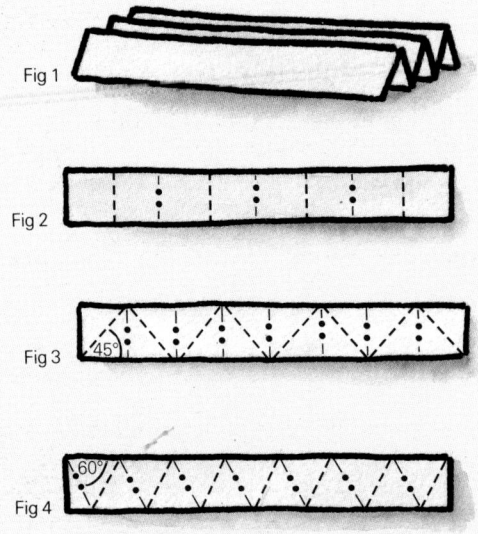

All designs start with some form of accordion pleat (see Fig 1). For dip dyeing, fold the pleat into smaller shapes (see Figs 2, 3 and 4). The broken lines represent valley folds, or creases which recede, and the dot-and-dash lines represent mountain folds, which come forward.

1 Make an accordion pleat (see Fig 1) with your chosen lightweight paper – colored tissue paper is ideal. Now fold as in Fig 2, 3 or 4, or experiment with your own folding ideas.

2 Pour some coloring – liquid watercolor, colored ink, food coloring or the like – into a shallow container (preferably one that will not stain) and dip either a corner or an edge of the folded paper into it. Allow the paper to absorb the color and let it spread a little.

3 Squeeze the excess liquid from the paper between paper towels or newsprint. Continue to color the folded paper as much as you wish. At this stage the wet tissue is very fragile.

4 Unfold the paper so that it forms a long pleated strip. Place this strip on some scrap paper, cover it with more scrap paper and either rub hard all along the strip or, preferably, use a roller. This removes a great deal of the excess moisture.

TIPS

- For softer-edged effects first dip the paper into water and squeeze it out before coloring it.
- Be careful not to transfer any color to the base of the iron; this is more likely to happen if the paper is still wet.

5 Now unfold the paper completely. Take care not to tear the tissue. Move the paper as little as possible at this stage and allow it to dry. When it is dry it can be ironed to remove some of the crease marks.

Below These dip-dyed examples show a variety of methods: use of wetted paper (left); felt pen technique (top right); wetted paper completely dyed (center right); and use of dry paper (bottom right).

ALTERNATIVES

It is also possible to draw patterns into the folded shapes, using felt-tipped pens. When the paper has been folded, dip it in water and squeeze it gently so that it is damp, not dripping. The felt pens will now easily penetrate several layers of paper. Open the folds partially to check how far through the layers the color has seeped, and rework the pattern from the faintest layer outward. Fat felt tips give bold results, whereas fine felt tips give delicate and more detailed patterns. Dry as for the basic method already described.

Below right These finished examples show different ways of pleating: straight pleating of colored tissue paper (left); diagonal pleating (top right); and repleating (bottom right).

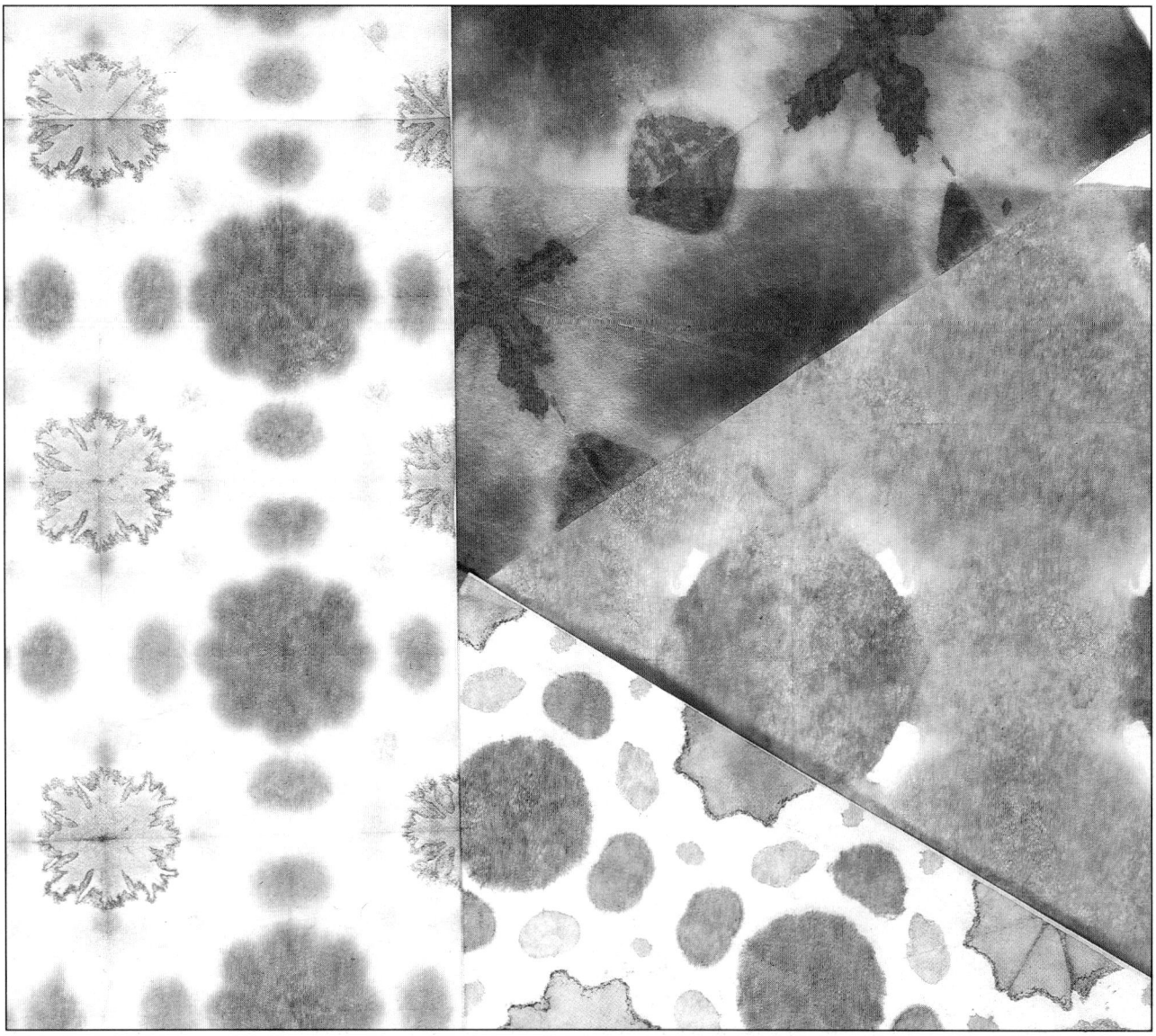

PLEATING

A method related to folding and dyeing is pleating and painting. There are many ways to pleat a piece of paper (see Figs 5–8 for some ideas). When the paper is pleated, hold the edges together on one side with bulldog clips, and paint the edges on the other side (see Fig 9). Repeat the process for the opposite edges. Dry as for the basic method. It is possible to repleat another design – checks or chevrons, for example – when the paper has dried, and to paint it again.

The finished papers are extremely decorative and can be used for many other projects: greeting cards, see pages 104–5; wrapping gifts, see pages 88–9; papier mâché decoration, see pages 54–6. The tissue paper can be mounted onto a sheet of lightly glued paper or board. It could be used in this form for lining envelopes, see page 106, and as a cover for a stationery holder, see pages 109–14 or a notepad.

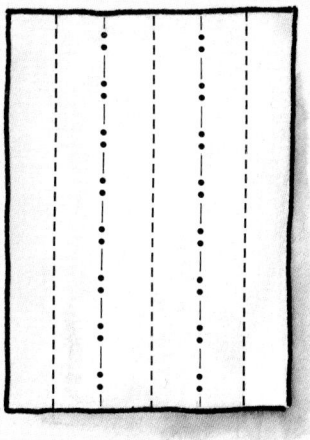

Fig 5

Fig 6

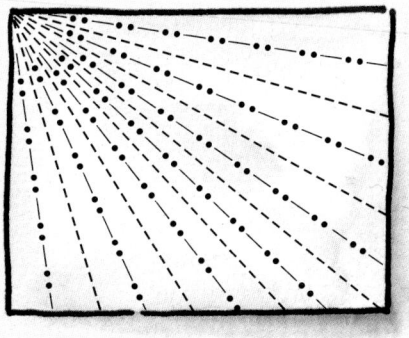

Fig 7

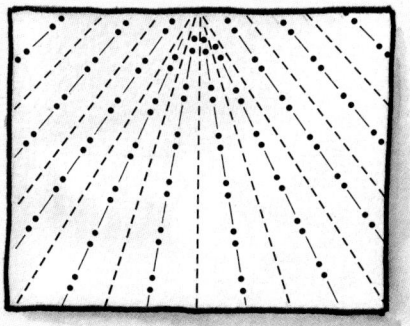

Fig 8

Fig 9

MARBLING

EQUIPMENT

- Shallow tray (photographer's tray or roasting dish)
- Wallpaper paste and mixing bowl
- Oil colors
- Turpentine or white spirit (mineral spirit)
- Ox-gall (available from well-stocked artists' supply stores)
- Jars for colors
- Old newspapers
- Sticks or knitting needles, for stirring
- Medicine dropper or pipette
- Card
- Double-sided adhesive tape
- Ruler
- Pencil
- Pins

The technique of marbling, by which paper is given a marbled pattern, is thought to have been invented in eastern Europe in the 16th century. The process relies on the fact that oil and water do not mix. Oil colors are floated on size or water, the paper is laid on the surface of the liquid, and when it is lifted off, picks up the pattern of the colors. It is a simple technique but needs practice to achieve consistent patterns. However, do not be deterred because it is a most enjoyable craft to practice, and even your first experiments will be presentable.

Marbled papers are mainly associated with bookbinding, but these days they appear on many household accessories: lamps and lampshades, candlesticks, wastepaper baskets, stationery holders and boxes, etc. Some marbled papers are now printed, but these do not usually have the quality – both visually and texturally – of handmade ones.

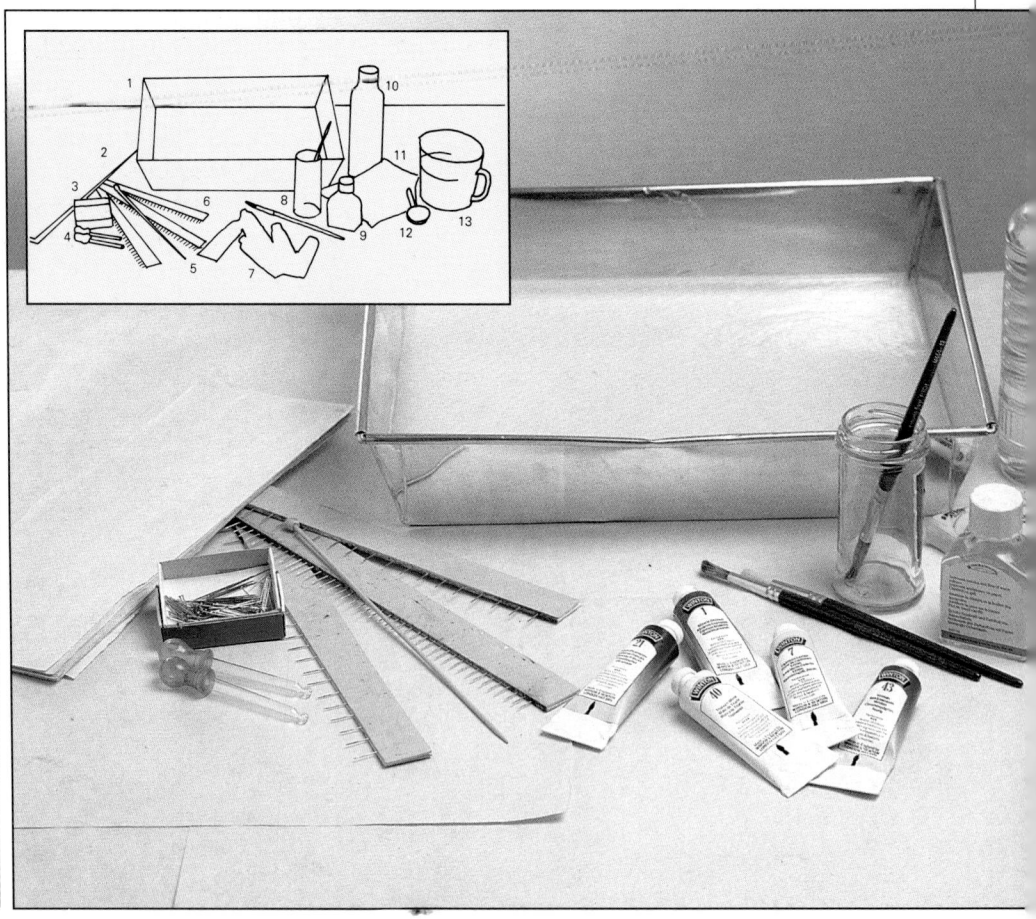

PREPARING THE BATH

Using approximately one heaped tablespoon to 4 cups of hot (not boiling) water, mix about one-quarter of the water with the paste (also known as size) in the tray until the paste is smooth. Then add the rest of the water, stirring well so that the size is free of lumps. Allow the mixture to stand for a while and prepare the colors.

Marbling can be done with a single color, particularly if you are using colored paper, but two or three colors can also be used. Squeeze out some oil paint onto a saucer or a palette. Add some turpentine or white spirit (mineral spirit) and stir continuously until the colors are thinned to a runny consistency. Then transfer the colors to individual jars.

The next step is the most uncertain part of the process and will probably require several attempts. Add ox-gall to the colors in order to reduce the surface tension and to allow the colors to spread on the size. Ox-gall reacts differently with each color, depending on factors such as the temperature of the room and the size, the consistency of the colors, etc. Start by adding five drops of ox-gall to two teaspoons of each color. If colors are being placed on top of each other, the second color will need additional ox-gall. However, you can make these adjustments during the marbling session.

Make sure that you have plenty of strips of newspaper or newsprint prepared for skimming excess color from the surface of the size. The strips should be slightly shorter than the tray and approximately 3 in wide.

Having completed these basic preparations, it is now time to start experimenting with the consistencies and temperatures of the size and the oil colors. Test each color individually (see chart) before attempting to use two colors or more together.

EQUIPMENT

1 Shallow tray
2 Lightweight to mediumweight paper
3 Pins
4 Medicine droppers
5 Knitting needle
6 Marbling combs (see page 50)
7 Oil colors
8 Mixing jar
9 Ox-gall
10 White spirit (mineral spirit)
11 Wallpaper paste
12 Measuring spoons
13 Measuring cup

TEST CHART

CAUTION It is essential that you skim the surface of the size with the strips of paper between each trial so that you can see clearly how the oil colors are reacting and also to get into the habit of skimming the surface between patterns.

- If the color disperses too thinly, there is too much ox-gall and you will have to add more thinned color.
- If the color does not spread, there is not enough ox-gall – add more, drop by drop. If this does not work, it is possible that the size is too thick and more water should be stirred in carefully.
- If the color sinks through the size, it usually means that the size is too thick and should therefore be thinned.
- If the color still sinks, the temperature of the size may not be right. If the size feels warmer than room temperature, then add cold water to it, and if it feels colder, add warm water.

BASIC METHOD

1 Having achieved all the right consistencies, it is time to make a pattern. Drop color randomly from a brush, loaded with color, tapped against the side of the tray. Repeat with more colors, if desired.

2 Using a stick or knitting needle, draw patterns in the size by dragging the implement through the oil colors. Take care to work only on the surface of the size and move the pattern-making implement gently and fairly slowly so that you disturb the bath as little as possible.

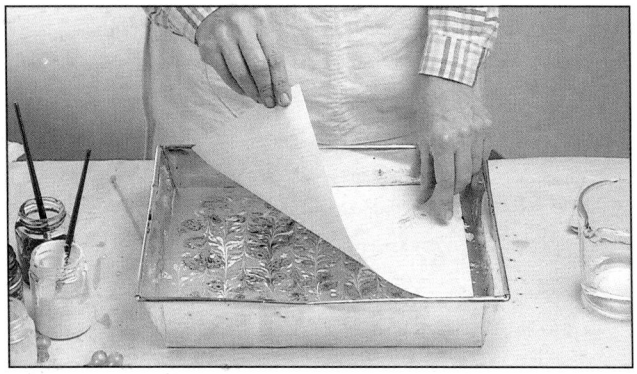

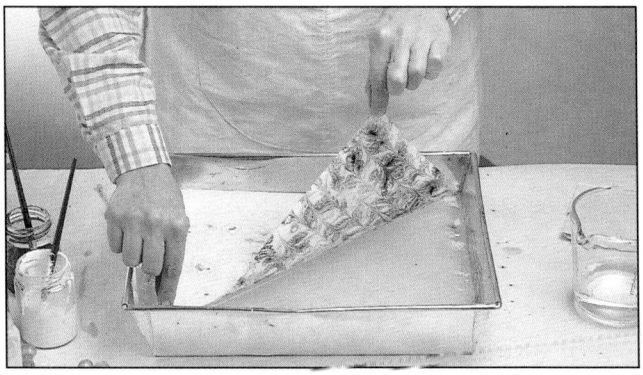

3 When the pattern looks satisfactory, take a piece of lightweight to mediumweight paper by the opposite corners and lay it onto the size carefully, with a rolling movement. Do this fairly slowly or else air bubbles will become trapped beneath the paper, forming unintended white spaces in the pattern.

4 Lift off the paper almost immediately by picking up two adjacent corners and peeling it off the surface of the size.

5 Let it drain on the side of the tray for a minute or so and then lay it on some newspaper to dry. If you wish, you can rinse the paper very gently to remove the excess size, but this can affect the color and is not really necessary. It is also possible to hang the paper on a line to dry.

CAUTION!!

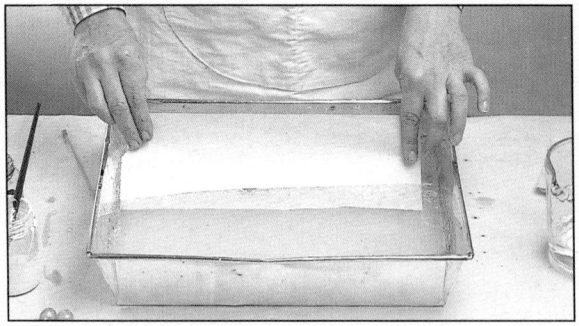

Remember to clean the excess color from the surface of the size before you start to create the next pattern. Lay a sheet of clean paper onto the paste mixture to soak up any remaining color.

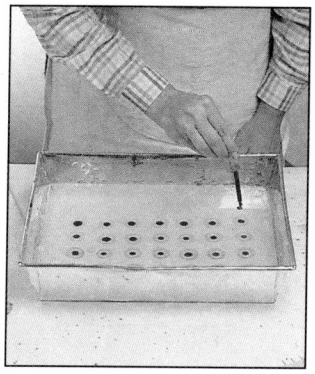

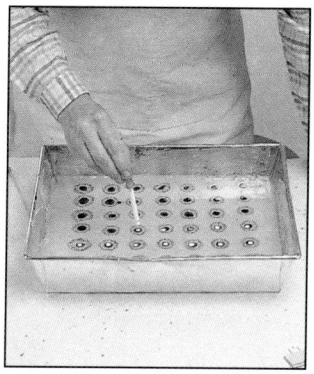

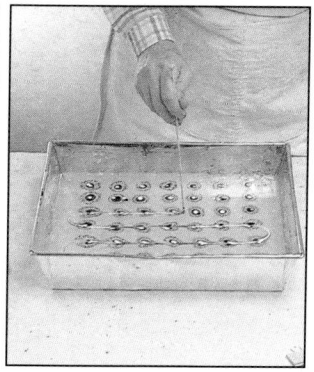

DESIGN VARIATIONS

1a Drop color onto the size with a dropper (**far left**).

1b Repeat, dropping further colors onto the first color (**center left**).

1c With a knitting needle, draw through the center of the dots to make a continuous thread (**left**).

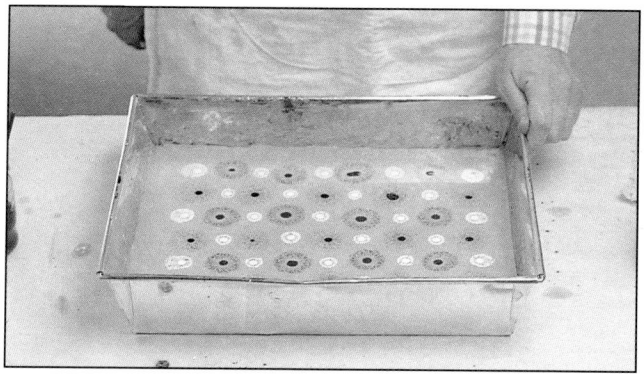

2a Alternatively, intersperse different colored drops of paint on the size.

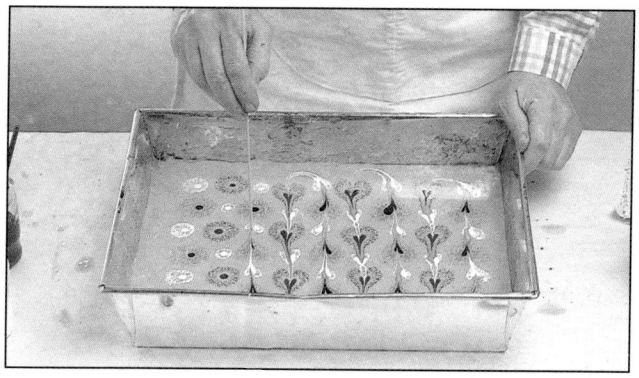

2b Draw down through the rows of dots to feather the colors and create a design.

2c Agitate the surface slightly with the needle to make the lines of color wavy.

2d Lay the paper slowly down onto the size.

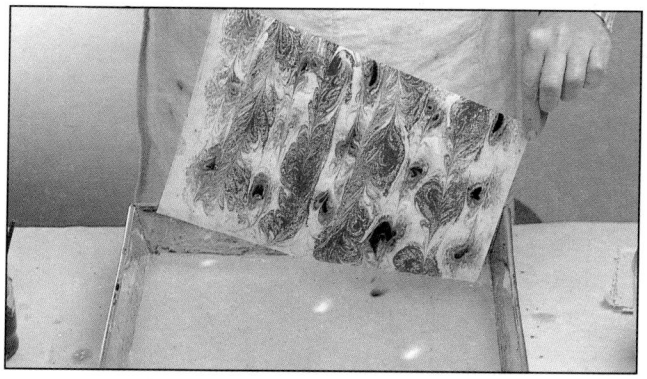

2e Quickly lift the paper off.

3a Alternatively, use larger movements to swirl the colors.

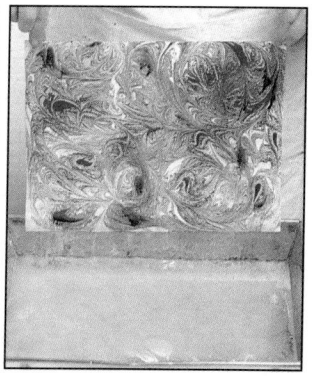

3b This produces a bolder, spiral design.

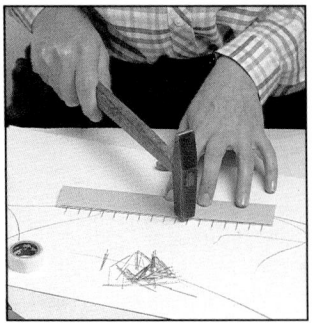

HOW TO MAKE A MARBLING COMB

1 Take two strips of card ½ in shorter than the width and/or length of the tray, and about 2 in wide. Mark off ½-in spaces on one strip.

2 Cover the edge of the strip with double-sided adhesive tape.

3 Position long pins on the tape at the marked points. Stick more tape to the other piece of card and stick the two cards together carefully.

4 Bang the two pieces firmly together with a hammer so that the cards are firmly stuck together. Additional combs can be made, setting different spaces for the teeth.

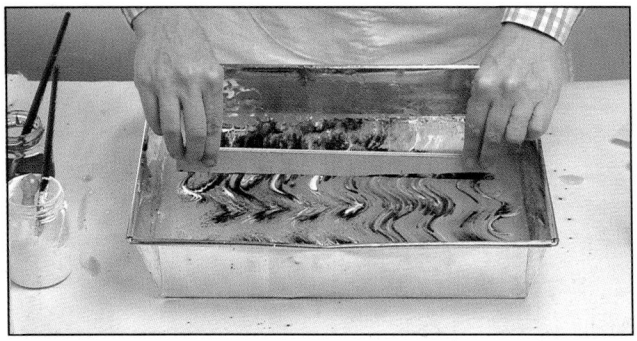

5 Drag the comb lightly through the color on the size, shifting it slightly as you do so to make a wavy pattern.

Below Some decorative examples using these marbling techniques on colored as well as white paper.

PAPIER MACHE

EQUIPMENT

- Old newspapers
- Colored tissue paper
- Wallpaper paste or thinned PVA adhesive
- Mold
- Petroleum jelly or plastic film
- Scissors
- Sandpaper
- Paint brushes
- Undercoat
- Decorating materials and varnish

The craft (some would say art) of making objects out of papier mâché is almost as old as papermaking and was first practiced by the Chinese. The objects they produced were pactical and decorative, and were often made especially for festivals, when they were painted with religious images. In the 18th century, papier mâché had a resurgence of popularity in Europe and was used for many household pieces, from trays and boxes to tables and chairs, which were often highly decorated. Nowadays papier mâché is frequently used for theater props, because it is simple to construct, lightweight, and, combined with modern epoxy glues, incredibly strong.

The term *papier mâché* is French and means "chewed-up paper." This describes the process very clearly: paper is torn into small pieces, glued and laid onto a mold. Several layers of paper are built up and, when the shape is thoroughly dry, it is removed from the mold, sanded smooth and decorated.

An alternative method is to make a papier mâché pulp or mash. It is complicated to prepare, but very easy to use. However, commercial brands are now available for home use. In this book the basic "strip and glue" method has been used.

BASIC METHOD

Prepare the working area by covering the table with newspaper. If you are using wallpaper paste, mix it according to the directions on the box; if you are using PVA adhesive, dilute it with three-parts glue to one-part water.

Choose a mold with no underlip, otherwise it will be impossible to remove the finished object. Now cover the mold with petroleum jelly or plastic film, so that the papier mâché object can be removed easily when the layers are dry.

TIPS

- One way of keeping track of the completed layers is to use different types of paper for alternate layers – such as newspaper and colored tissue paper. Eight layers is a good average for most articles.
- Depending on the object, it may be wise to make the base thicker; for example, a wastepaper basket would benefit from the extra strength and weight of a thicker base.
- The larger the article the longer it will take to dry.

1 Having torn up the newspaper and tissue, dampen the pieces, and lay neatly on the mold.

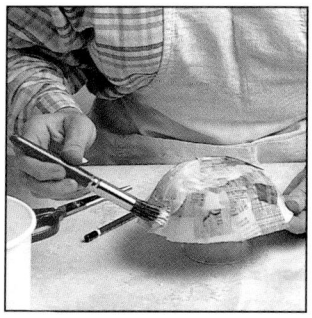

2 When the mold is covered, paint the surface liberally with the thinned adhesive or paste.

3 Now add the next layer.

4 When the mold is covered with this layer, brush on more adhesive. For a smooth result, try to work methodically so that the mold is covered evenly.

5 Put the mold in a warm place and leave it to dry for about 24 hours. Remove the shape from the mold carefully.

6 If necessary, trim the edges of the shape.

7 If the edge feels uneven or thin, it is possible to build up the shape at this stage.

8 Using medium- to fine-grade sandpaper, sand the article smooth and then paint it with two layers of undercoat. This ensures that the object has an even base on which to apply the final decoration.

Left There are many possibilities for decorating the finished object: you could apply collage or stencil a design onto it, see pages 34–7, or draw or paint onto it directly.

DECORATING PAPIER MACHE

BOWL 1 This bowl has such an open shape that the outside is barely visible. Therefore, it is painted in a single color and the inside is decorated.

2 Cut a piece from a sheet of folded and dyed Japanese paper. Apply thinned PVA adhesive to the base of the bowl. Place the cutout in position and press down gently as the dye may not be permanent and may spread.

3 Cut circles from colored tissue paper and stick them round the edge of the bowl. Again take care when sticking these in position that the color does not run.

4 When the first layer of circles is tacky, position the smaller circles and paint over them with another layer of PVA adhesive, which acts as a varnish. It is possible to use many overlapping layers of colored tissue and work on a colored background, which will affect the colors of the tissue. Try out various designs, using colored paper for experiments.

Left The finished bowl, complete with decoration, makes an attractive container.

PLANT POT HOLDER

1 First spray the plant pot holder with a layer of paint and then decorate with leaf stencils. Make the stencils from lightweight paper so that they can be curved around the shape easily. Attach them to the holder with small pieces of plastic putty.

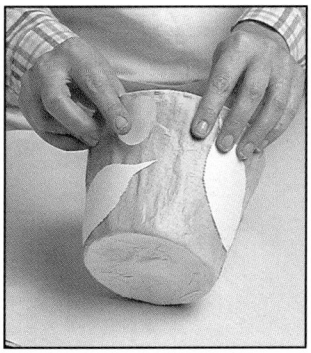

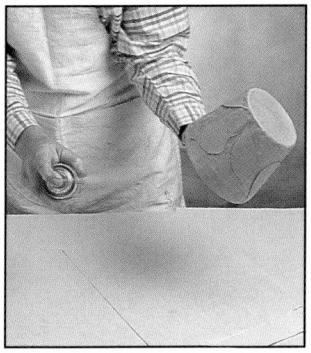

2 Now, in a well-ventilated space, spray the holder with another layer of paint. You can achieve the same effect by painting onto the object with a brush.

Left Remove the stencils and apply varnish to the internal and external faces of the pot holder to make it waterproof. Leave the inside undecorated as it will be hidden by the plant.

WASTEPAPER BASKET
1 Decorate the outside of the basket with a collage of torn paper strips of newspaper and thin black paper.

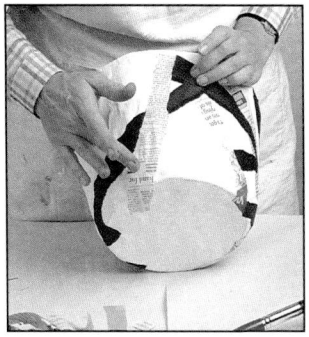

2 Paste the strips and then position randomly around the basket

3 Trim the strips to fit, cutting them flush with the top of the basket but allowing them to overlap at the bottom.

Left Varnish the inside of the basket or cover with a layer of enamel paint. The end result is original and effective, and simply achieved.

ORIGAMI

Origami is a Japanese word which comes from the words *ori* (to fold) and *kami* or *gami* (paper). It was in Japan that the art first originated, some 1400 years ago. In its purest form, origami can be defined as the art of manipulating a paper square without the paper being cut, pasted, decorated or mutilated in any way; it may only be folded. This restrictive rule makes origami the most refined of all paper arts, but therein lies its beauty and wide appeal.

Only a few dozen traditional Japanese designs have come down to us, such as the flapping bird, crane, jumping frog or waterbomb (balloon). During the 1930s, though, the founding genius of modern origami – Akira Yoshizawa – came to realize that the art had enormous creative potential. Following his example, many other people around the world have created tens of thousands of new designs, some elegantly simple, others enormously complex. The designs range from animals to manmade objects and from expressive abstract forms to geometric solids.

Origami enthusiasts like to form clubs and to teach and take classes. Many adult education programs offer beginning and advanced origami classes. Check the course announcements in your local newspaper and at community centers such as YMCAs. If no course is being offered, suggest the idea to the program director.

The designs that follow were originated by Paul Jackson, with the exception of the Printer's Hat and Japanese Box, both of which are traditional.

PAPER

Specialist shops often sell packets of square, thin origami paper from Japan, brightly colored on one side and white on the reverse. These papers are convenient to use, but can sometimes be expensive. Artists' supply stores and good stationers occasionally sell locally manufactured origami paper at a better price, though quality cannot be guaranteed.

If you are unable to buy special origami paper, any paper which can take a crease without cracking or unfolding is suitable. Good papers for practicing on include typing paper, writing paper, brown wrapping paper, photocopy paper or computer paper. For making origami displays the best papers include gift-wrap papers (useful because they have a pattern or color on one side and are white on the other), colored photocopy paper and any attractive papers and paper-backed metallic foils found in artists' supply stores or stationers. Even thicker water-absorbent papers such as Ingres (Strathmore) paper or watercolor paper are suitable if lightly dampened before folding. Unsuitable papers are newspaper, paper towels, tissues and coated papers such as poster paper, as the colored pigment cracks when folded.

If you cannot find papers with a different color on either side, lay two different colored sheets back to back and fold them as one layer. Do not glue them together.

SYMBOLS

These symbols are the ABC of origami and will enable you to make the designs which follow. Until you become familiar with them, keep referring back to this page. In particular, look at the different types of arrow.

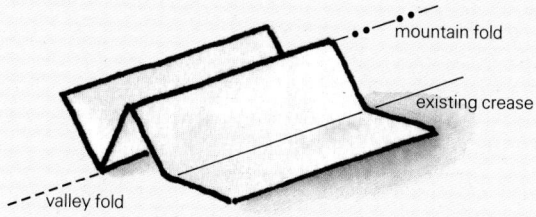

Simple folds and creases

Fold to the front, or to the side

Fold behind

Fold, placing one spot on the other

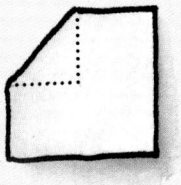

X-ray view

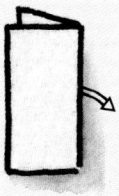

Unfold crease(s)

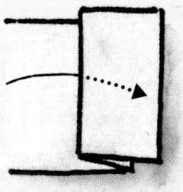

Fold under or inside

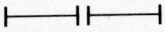

Equal distances

TIPS ON FOLDING

- Where possible, always fold against a hard, smooth surface such as a table or hard-backed book. Folding in the air is recommended for experts, but is difficult for beginners.
- Follow the instructions carefully, looking closely at the drawings and reading the captions. Take particular note of the lettered corners.
- Remember that the folds you are asked to make in one drawing will give you a shape which looks like the next drawing, so keep looking ahead to see what you are trying to achieve.
- Fold slowly and neatly. Some designs will take a little practice, so be ready to make them a few times before they look good.

PRINTER'S HAT

1 Begin with a double-page sheet from a broadside (large format) newspaper. Fold it in half from top to bottom. Then take the left edge to the right. Crease and unfold. Fold the top corners down to the center crease.

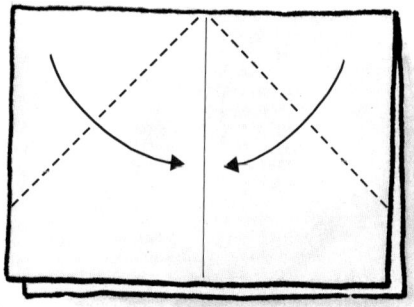

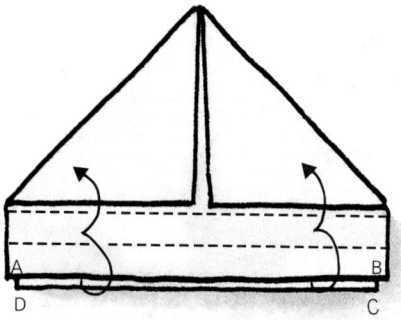

2 Fold the top layer edge AB up to the base of the triangles, then fold it up again along the base of the triangles . . .

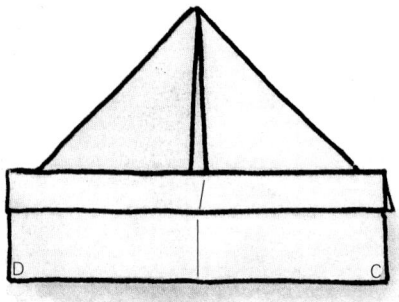

3 . . . to look like this. Turn the shape over.

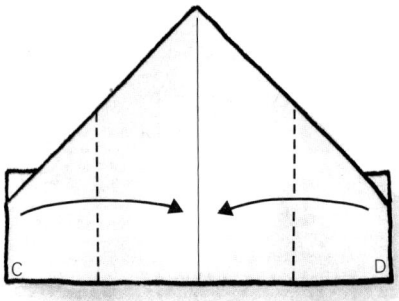

4 Fold the left and right edges C and D in to the center crease.

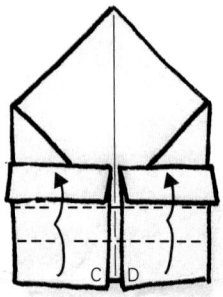

5 As in step 2, fold up the bottom edge CD to the base of the folds, and then fold them up again along the base of the folds.

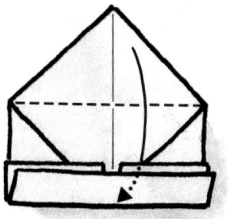

6 Fold down the top corner, tucking it underneath all the layers at the bottom.

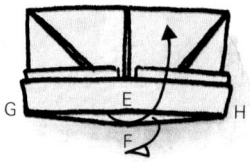

7 Separate E from F . . .

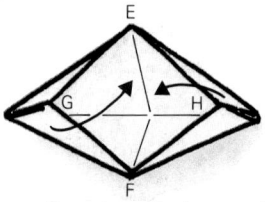

8 . . . pulling them further and further apart so that G and H come together . . .

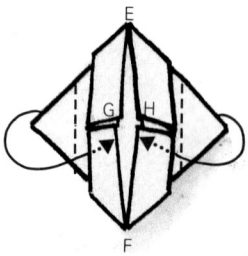

9 . . . in the middle. Flatten the shape into a square and crease the edges. Fold the right and left corners into the middle and tuck under the layers at G and H (**left**).

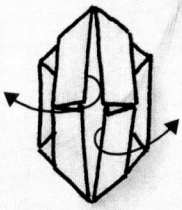

10 Open up the shape and square off the sides.

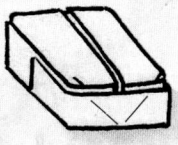

11 The complete Printer's Hat.

BUTTERFLY

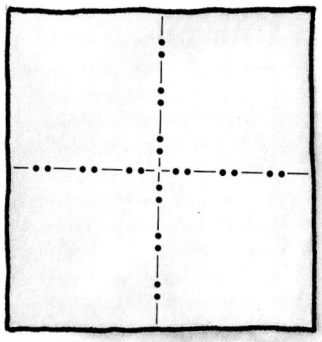

1 Make horizontal and vertical mountain creases.

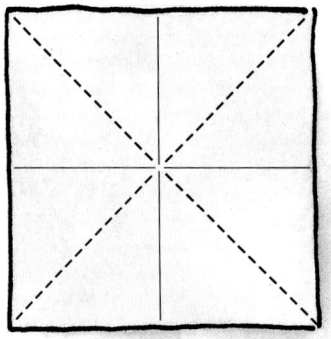

2 Make diagonal valley folds.

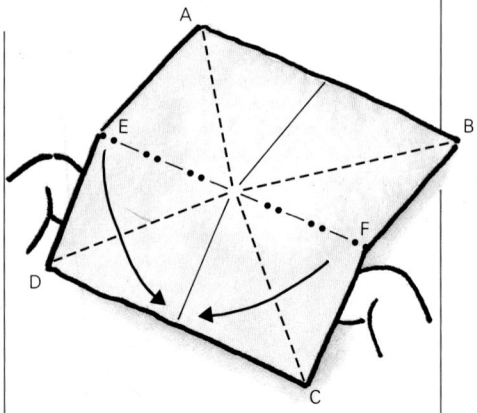

3 With DC on the table and AB up in the air, place your fingers behind E and F and pull them up and inward . . .

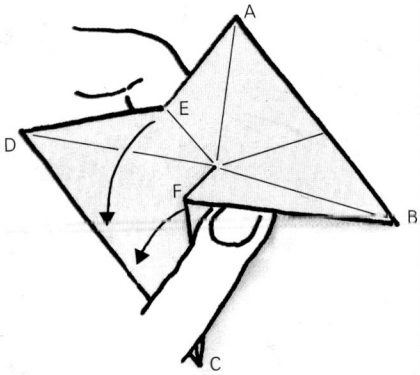

4 . . . like this, so that they lie together in the middle of edge DC . . .

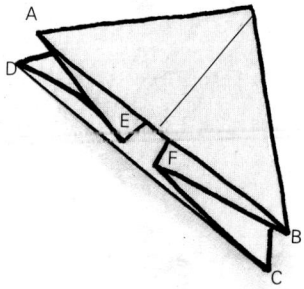

5 . . . like this. Note how A lies on D and B on C.

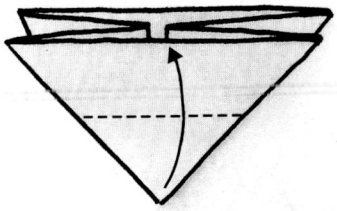

6 Turn the triangle upside down and fold the bottom corner up to the top edge.

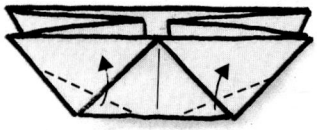

7 Fold in the bottom corners as shown.

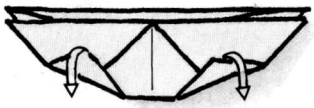

8 Unfold the corners.

9 Fold the bottom corners in again, but this time crease only the inner layers. Much of the crease is hidden inside the outer layer. Look at step 10.

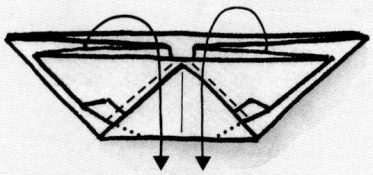

10 Pull down the top layer triangles.

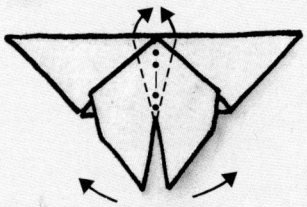

11 Make a central mountain crease, then two valley creases in the shape of a V, one on either side of the mountain. This pinches the center of the butterfly to create a raised body and separates the lower wings.

12 The complete butterfly.

CHATTERBOX

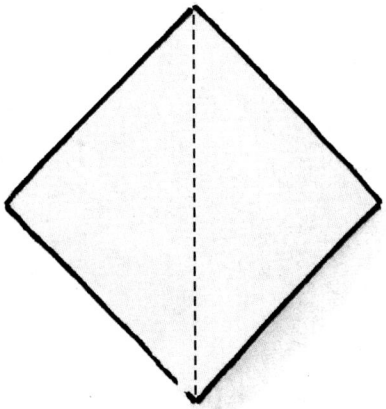

1 Make a valley fold along a vertical diagonal, and unfold

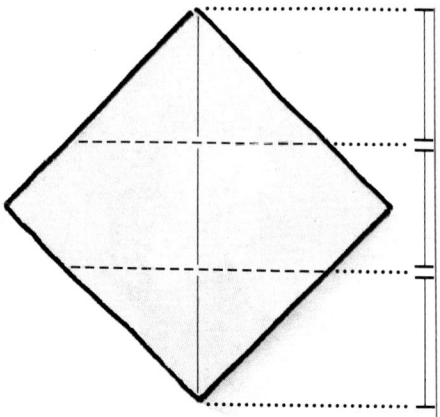

2 Carefully fold horizontal valley folds, which cross the diagonal crease at accurate thirds. Use a ruler to help you locate the creases. Unfold.

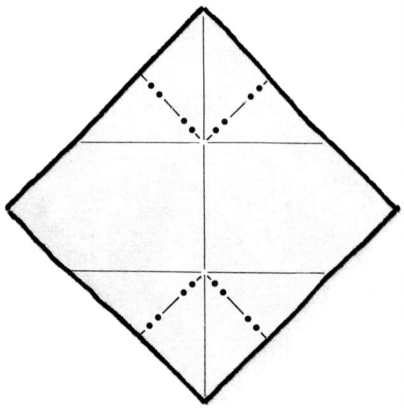

3 Make short mountain folds from the edges to the intersection of the steps 1 and 2 folds.

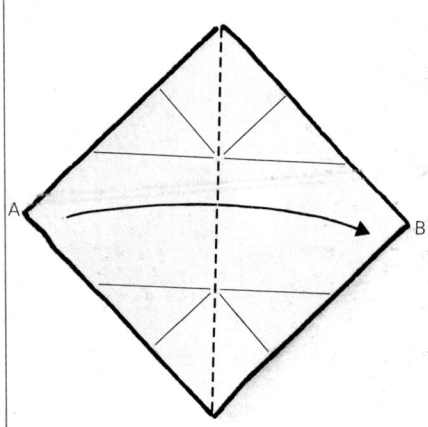

4 Fold the lefthand corner across to the right.

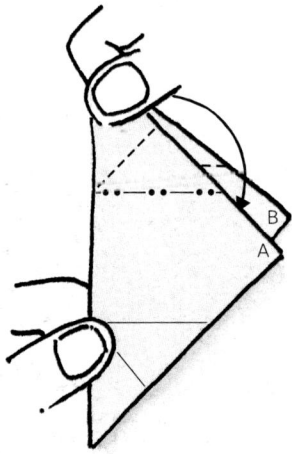

5 Grip the paper as shown. Push the top corner down in between layers A and B . . .

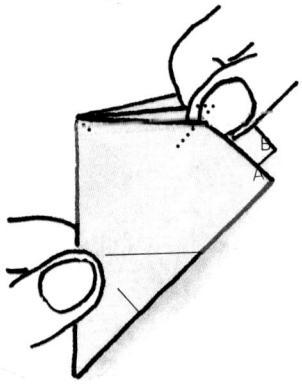

6 . . . like this. Flatten the paper.

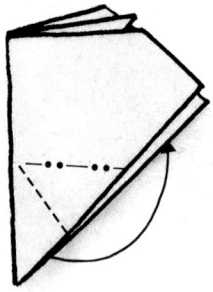

7 Repeat at the bottom.

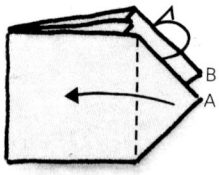

8 Fold A forward to the left, and take B behind to the left.

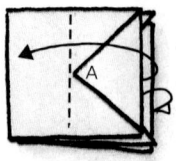

9 Take the upper right edge and fold it forward to the left edge; take the second right edge and fold it behind to the left edge, leaving the central spikes in place.

10 Fold the loose triangles in to the middle, two on the front, two on the back.

11 Partly unfold step 10, allowing the triangles to stand upright.

12 Draw in the eyes. Hold flap X at the front and back, one flap in each hand . . .

13 . . . and chatter away!

REPEAT PATTERN

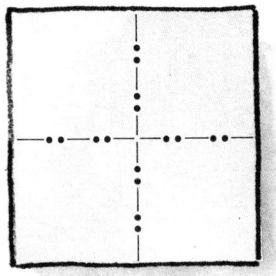

1 Make center mountain creases, horizontally and vertically.

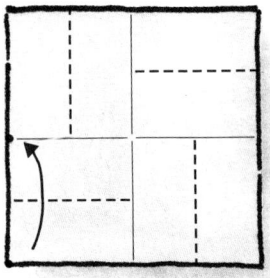

2 Fold the bottom edge of the paper up to the center horizontal crease, but only press flat the left half of the paper, making a crease from the lefthand edge into the center. Do this with all the other edges of the paper.

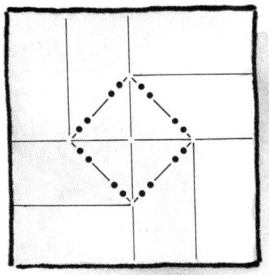

3 Make short diagonal mountain creases (or valley creases if you turn the paper over – this might be easier) connecting the points where steps 1 and 2 creases meet.

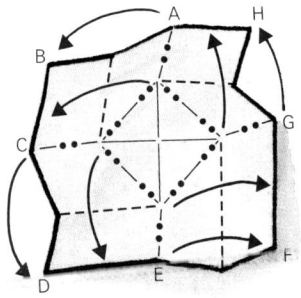

4 This step may be difficult, but persevere! Strengthen all creases. Simultaneously pinch the short mountain creases running into A, C, E and G and fold them over to corners B, D, F and H along the step 2 creases. This makes four pleats, contracts the paper and makes the center diamond shape twist anti-clockwise. All the creases move, twist and collapse together.

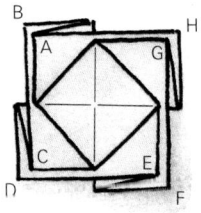

5 The flattened paper looks like this.

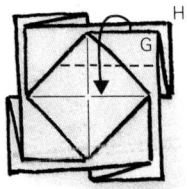

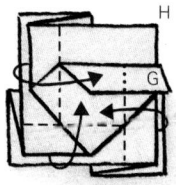

6 Bring the folded edge at the top of the paper (G) down to the center (**left**).

7 Repeat with the three other folded edges (**right**).

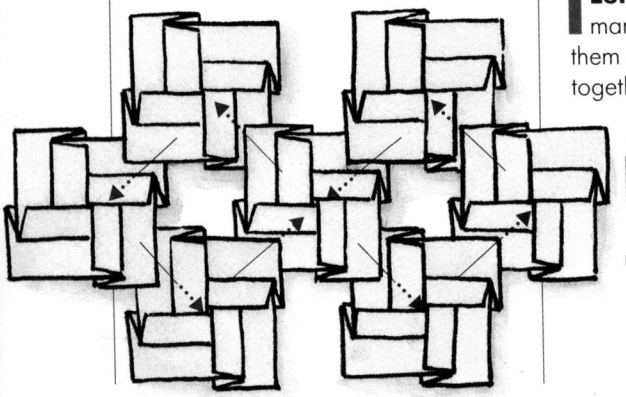

Left The complete unit. Make as many as you need and interlock them as shown, holding them together with glue.

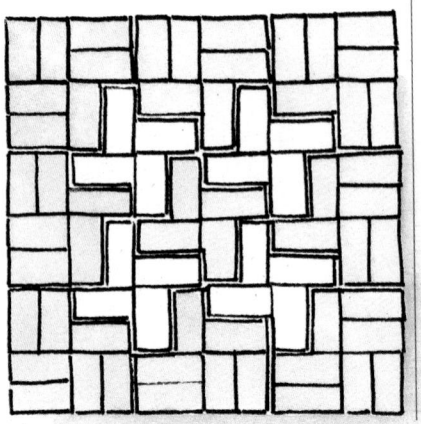

Right This diagram shows 13 units interlocked, four white and nine tinted. Your own patterns need not be so regular.

FISH No. 1

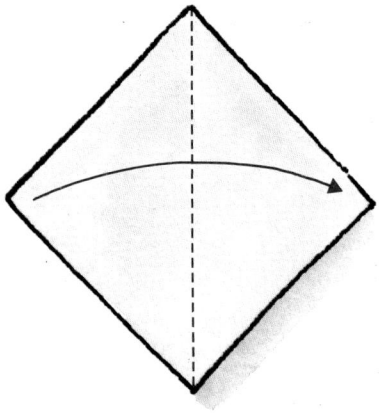

1 Valley fold the sheet in half along the vertical diagonal.

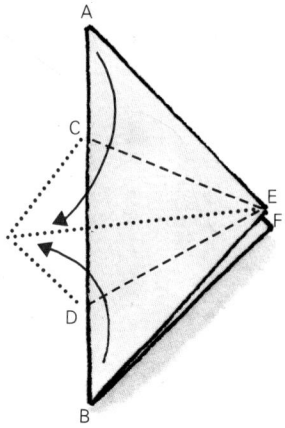

2 Fold corners A and B over to the left so that they touch. (Note that AC is longer than BD.)

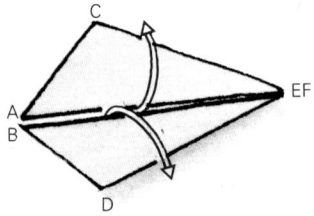

3 Unfold. (Note that triangle ACE is larger than BDE.)

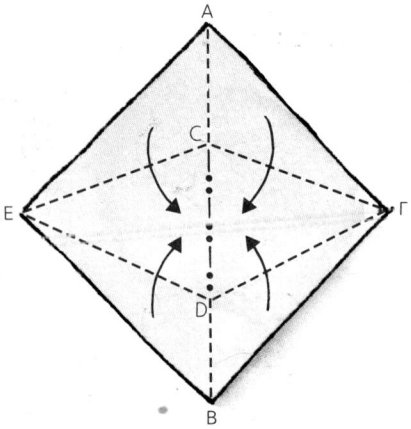

4 Refold all creases exactly as shown. Begin to fold along creases EC, CF, ED and DF, so that A and B come forward . . .

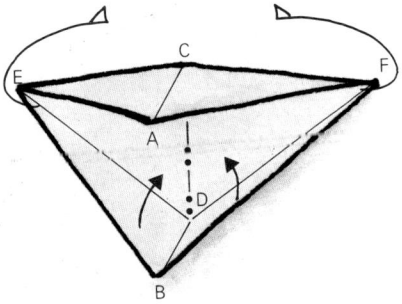

5 . . . like this. Bend E and F backward so that they meet. A and B also meet . . .

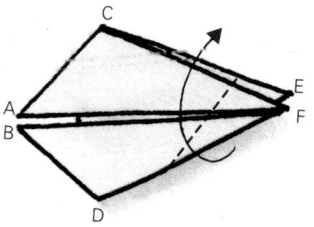

6 . . . like this. Fold up E and F as shown.

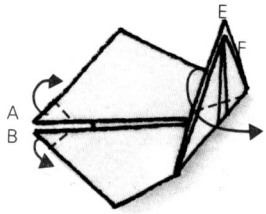

7 Pull down corner F to complete the tail. Turn corners A and B inside out, opening out each to do so.

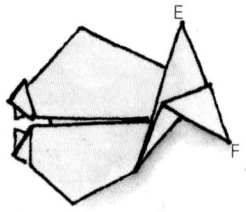

8 The complete fish . . .

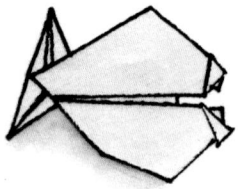

9 . . . and from the other side.

FISH No. 2

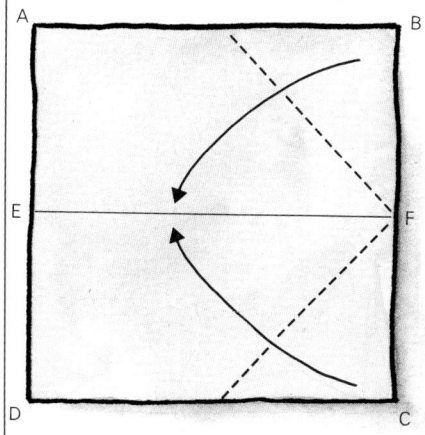

1 Fold a horizontal crease already made and unfold. Fold corners B and C in to the middle.

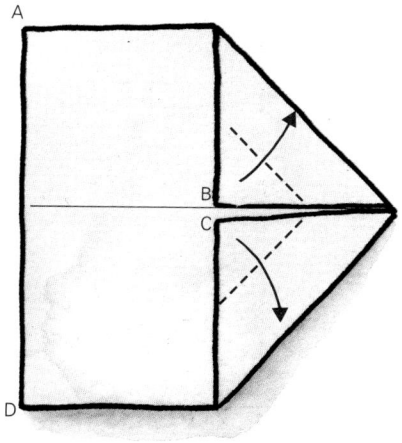

2 Fold B and C back out to the sloping edges.

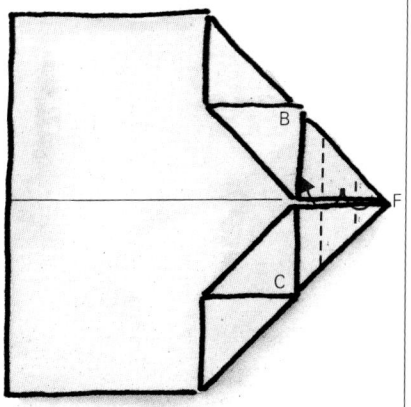

3 Fold corner F over twice to lie next to BC.

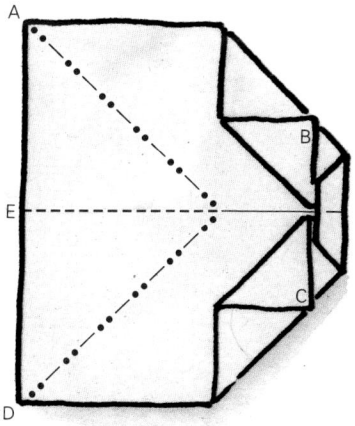

4 Carefully fold diagonal mountain folds, from corners A and D in to the middle and a horizontal valley fold from E to meet them. Begin to fold all three corners at once . . .

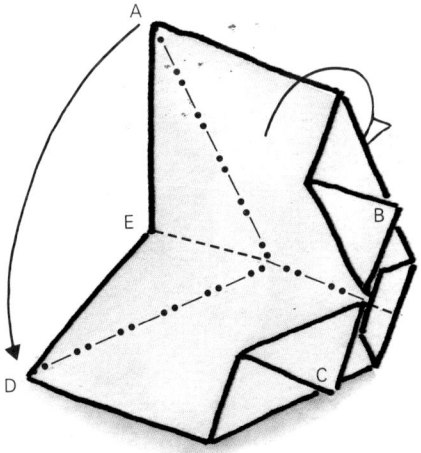

5 . . . so that the paper starts to collapse. A comes towards D. Note the mountain fold between B and C. Let A touch D.

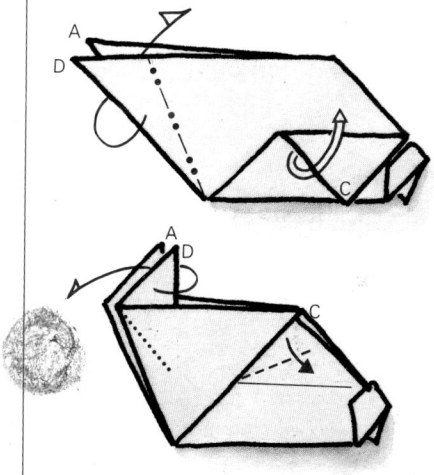

6 Fold D then A up through the center. Unfold C (and B behind) (**top**). Twist D back out. Fold C forward (and B behind) (**above**).

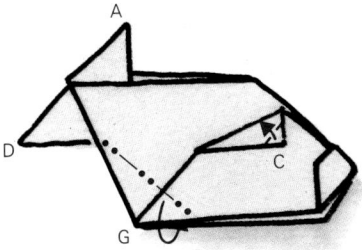

7 Fold back corner C to form an eye (and B behind). Push corner G under to the middle of the fish . . .

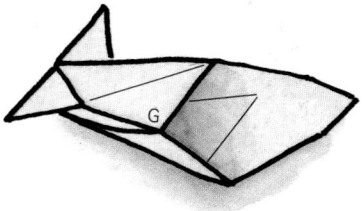

8 . . . to spread open the body, as seen here from underneath.

9 The complete fish.

HOW TO MAKE A MOBILE

A mobile is a wonderful way of displaying what you make, particularly if it follows a theme, such as a shoal of fish. Placed in moving air near a window or door, the fish will spin slowly, each wire moving independently of the others to create constantly changing arrangements of fish.

Although spectacular, mobiles are surprisingly easy to construct. You do, however, need to follow a few basic rules.

The horizontal wires should be thin and lightweight. Wire rods from florists or model shops are ideal and can easily be cut to length with pliers or a hacksaw. Wooden rods such as dowel or canes are usable, but can look clumsy. Cotton or fine fishing line can be used to suspend the fish.

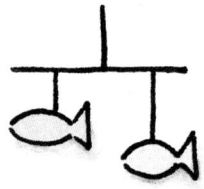

1 Attach lengths of thread to the balancing points of two origami fishes. Tie the other end of each thread to either end of a wire. Tie another thread tightly to the middle of that wire and slide it about until the wire is balanced exactly.

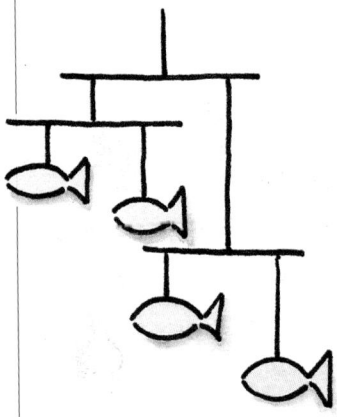

2 Repeat with another pair of fish. Attach each end of the loose threads to a wire, so that a pair of fish hang from each end. Attach a thread to the middle of the top wire and slide it about until the wire balances exactly.

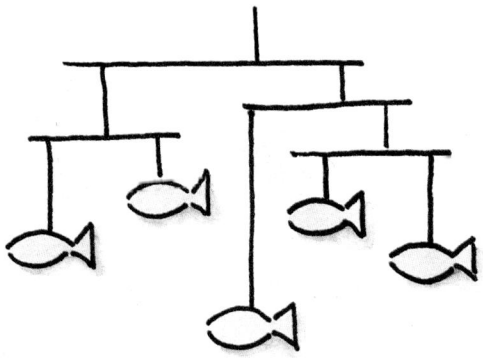

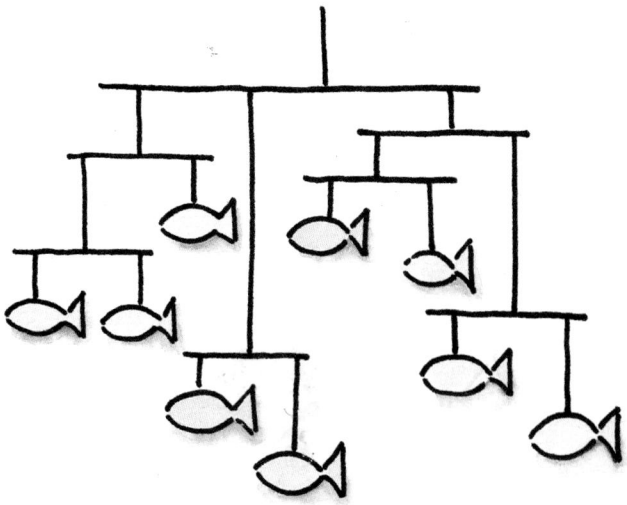

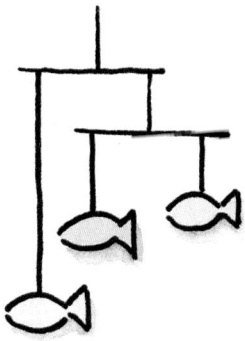

3 This process can be repeated as many times as you wish. Always design the mobile from the bottom up, making it balance at each level before progressing upward. Check that every fish can rotate through 360° without bumping into another.

JAPANESE BOX

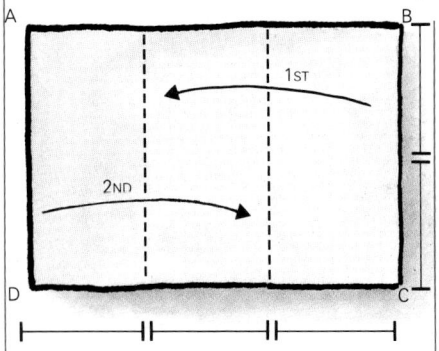

1 Begin with a 3 × 2 rectangle (one that measures three sections along one side to two sections along the adjacent side). Divide it into thirds, first folding BC across to the left, then fold AD across on top to the right.

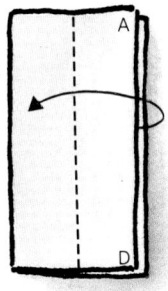

2 Fold AD back to the left edge.

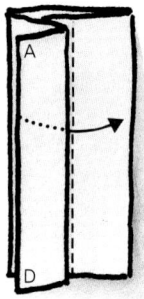

3 Pull out edge BC from under AD and fold it back to the right.

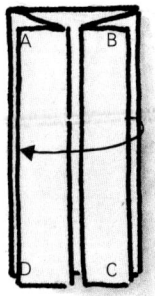

4 Unfold BC so that it meets and covers AD.

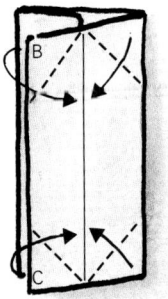

5 Turn in the four corners, the ones at B and C being single layers.

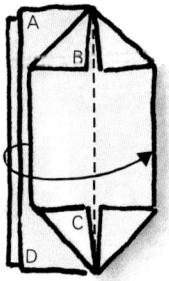

6 Fold BC back over to the right to meet the righthand edge.

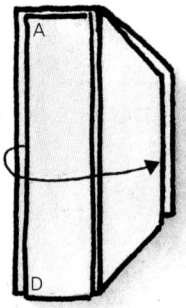

7 Unfold AD over to the right.

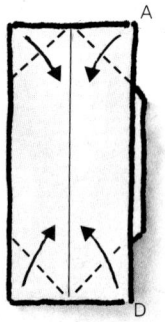

8 Turn in the four corners to meet the center crease.

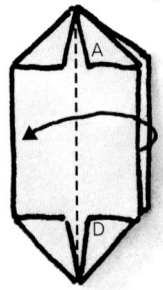

9 Fold AD back over to the left.

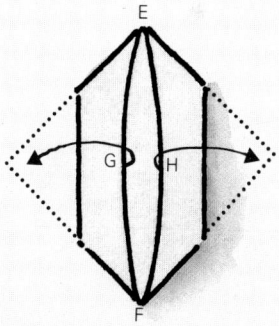

10 The paper is now symmetrical. Pull open the slit at G and H . . .

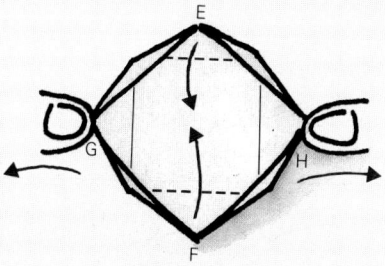

11 . . . opening up the box. Continue to pull so that as G and H separate, E and F come together in the middle . . .

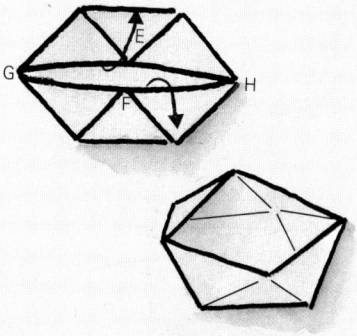

12 . . . like this. Open up EF a little (**top**). The Japanese box is now complete (**above**).

VALENTINE HEART

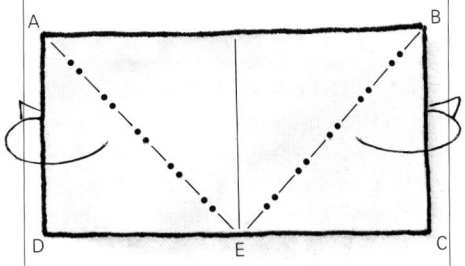

1 Begin with a 2 × 1 rectangle creased down the middle. Mountain fold corners C and D behind.

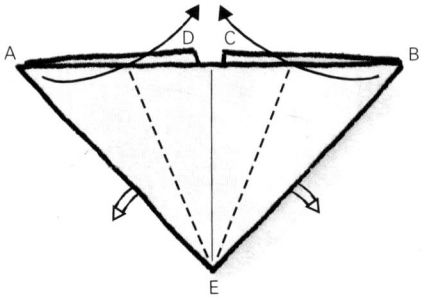

2 Fold edges AE and BE in to the center crease, allowing D and C to swivel downward and to the front . . .

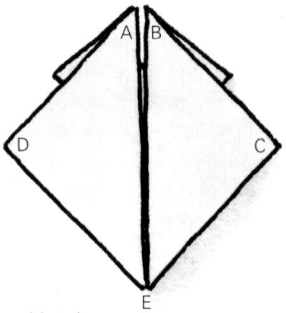

3 . . . like this. Turn over.

4 Fold B and A downward so that they lie at the folded edges running down to E.

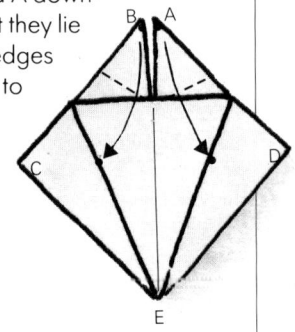

5 Tuck the loose corners into the pockets at B and A, locking B and A to the body of the paper. Fold in C and D as shown.

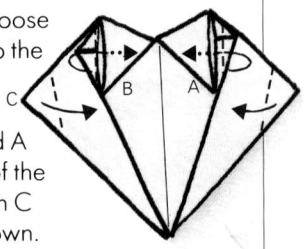

6 Turn over.

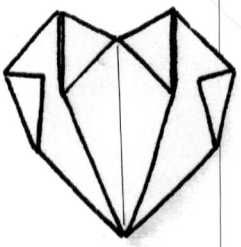

7 The complete Valentine heart.

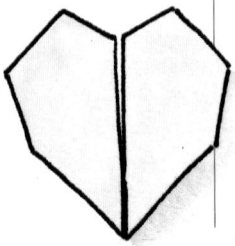

BOXES AND BAGS

EQUIPMENT

- Sharp pencil and ruler
- Knife and metal ruler
- Cutting mat or scrap board
- Scissors
- Bone folder (if possible)
- A pair of compasses
- Protractor and/or set squares
- Various glues
- Various adhesive tapes
- Thin card
- Paper

This chapter opens up almost endless possibilities and many of the ideas are easily carried out. The most inexpensive gift can be made to look very special in its own box, and gifts which are awkward to wrap effectively can have their own custom-made box or bag.

The boxes should be made from thin card and the bags from various weights of paper, see pages 8–13. If colored card (sometimes called board or art cover board) is not available, it is possible to glue gift-wrapping paper or decorated paper, see pages 32–50, to thin card. Make sure that the grain of both the card and the paper runs in the same direction, see page 9. Apply the glue evenly, but not excessively. Press the paper to remove any air bubbles.

When cutting curves you will achieve a smoother line if you keep the scissors in the same position while closing the blades slowly together and turning the card evenly with the other hand.

Score paper and card before you fold it because this helps to create a good crease. If possible, use a bone folder; otherwise, a blunt knife or the back of a scissors blade will do. If you are using a heavyweight card it may be necessary to cut through half the thickness of the card to achieve a good fold. Do this very carefully, using a craft knife or scalpel.

In order not to be wasteful, it may be wise for you to try out the more complicated boxes using paper first, before working on an expensive sheet of card. This is also a useful way of checking that the dimensions of the box are correct for the gift that you are planning to place within it.

In all the diagrams in this chapter the solid line should be cut and the dotted lines should be scored; a broken line represents a placement line. After you have removed the shape from its sheet and scored it, remember to fold all the lines to check the angles and the fit before you do any gluing. Small adjustments can often be made at this stage.

Glue flaps are used for all the projects in this chapter. They should be at least ½ in deep. If the shape is large, the glue flaps could be made up to 1 in deep. Tucking flaps are used on many of the boxes; these are always a little deeper than the glue flaps and can be cut at a more oblique angle to provide a tight fit.

Right These basic boxes were made from card which had been decorated using techniques described in the Decorating Paper chapter, see pages 32–50.

BASIC BOX

When drawing a plan for a basic box, work out the dimensions and, whatever the size, make sure that all angles are 90° (see Fig 1). The larger the box the thicker the card should be.

The number of flaps should equal the number of cut edges.

Use a sharp knife to cut out the shape, and cut away from the work – it would be infuriating to cut into the shape accidentally, having spent time carefully drawing it out.

Check the fit of the box, and stick the sides together, using a clear-drying, all-purpose adhesive, rather than a glue stick. Next, stick the base in position. The box is now complete.

If you are using plain card you could decorate the outside, or cover the card with gift-wrapping paper. It is best to decorate or cover the card before assembling the box.

It is possible to make the basic box collapsible. Add the glue flaps to the base instead of the bottom of the sides, and then stick only the side glue flap in position. The box can now be flattened and assembled when required. But remember that the box will not be as strong as a rigid one and do not forget to stick the base in place so that the bottom does not fall out of the box at the wrong moment!

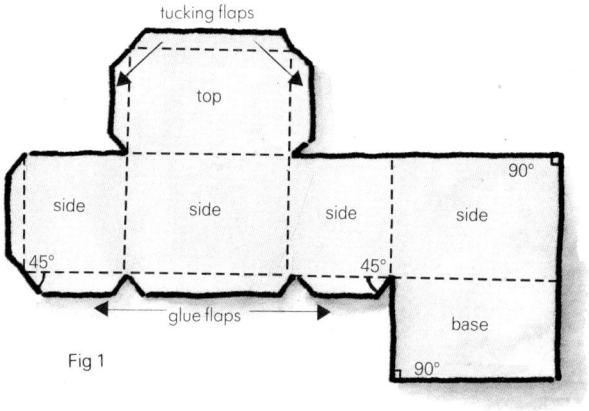

Fig 1

Above These three boxes were made from plain-colored card with different dimensions using the basic method.

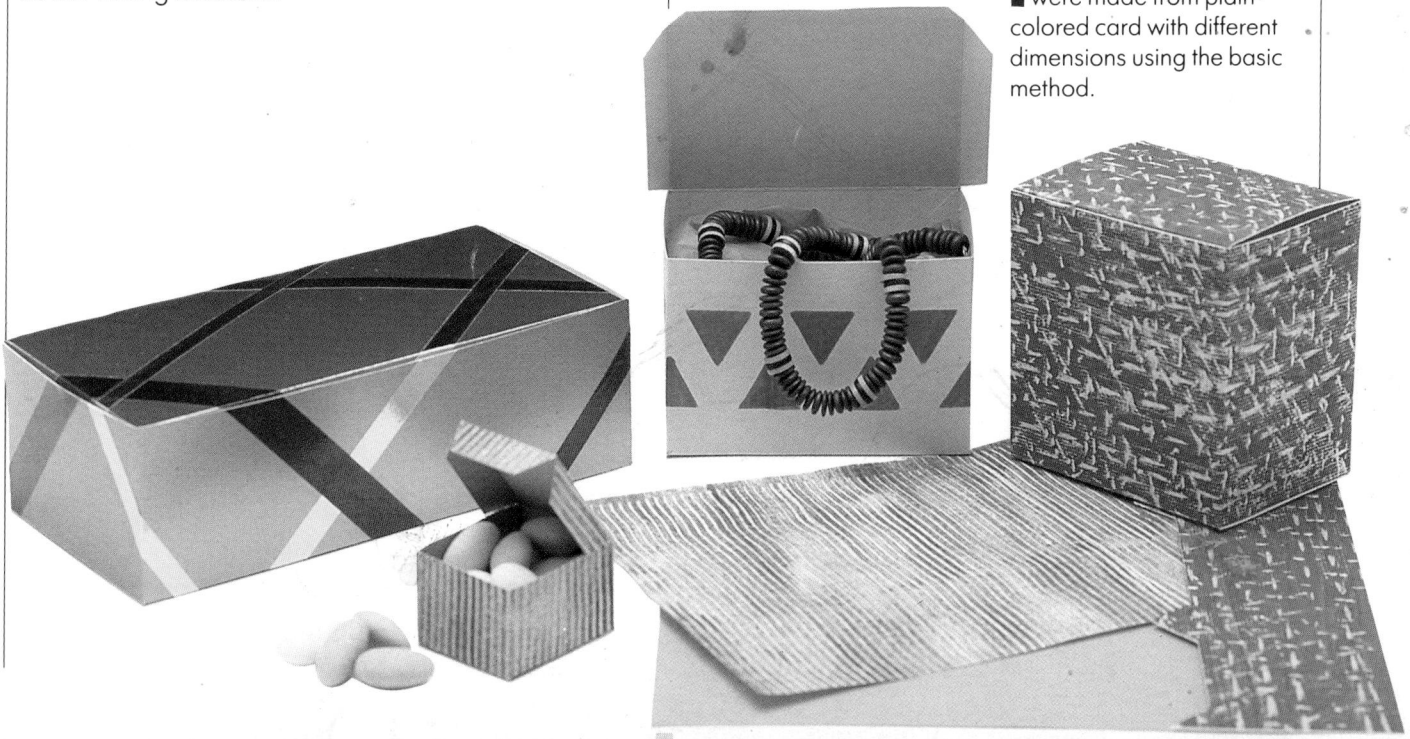

TWO-PIECE BOXES

A two-piece box can be as simple as the silver box in the photograph, or more complicated, like the red one with the star shape. A two-piece box is more economical to make than the basic box, but cannot be collapsed.

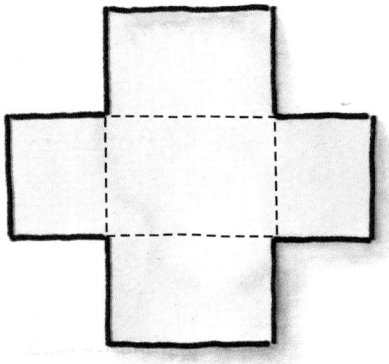

1a The easiest way to make a box with a separate lid is to cut out the box shape to the required size and to stick the sides together, using adhesive tape (decorated adhesive tape is very effective here).

1b Make the lid in exactly the same way, but make the sides very short; the dimensions of the rectangle should be 1/16 in larger in both directions to accommodate the thickness of the card.

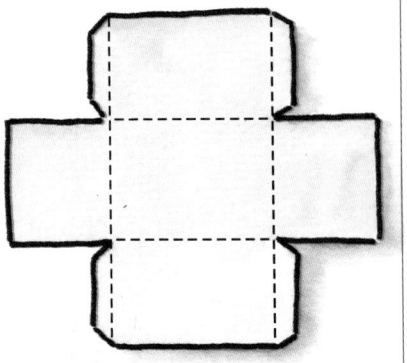

1c If adhesive tape is not suitable or available, the same result can be achieved by adding glue flaps. Make sure the allowance for the card thickness is generous when you are making the lid because the glue flaps will increase the thickness.

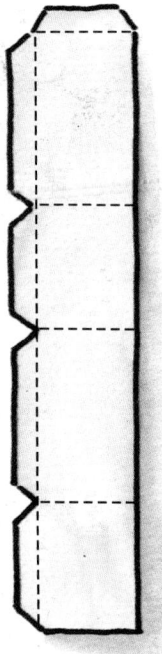

2a To make the blue box in the photograph, mark out a strip of card which is equal in length to twice the length and twice the width of the gift plus a glue flap, and equal to the height of the gift plus a glue flap. The strip can have joins if necessary. Cut out, score the folds and glue to form a box.

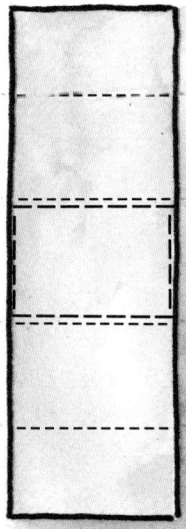

2b For the wrap-around lid, mark out a piece of card measuring the length of the gift by twice the width and twice the height plus an overlap. Cut out and score the folds.

2c Glue the center section of the lid to the glue flaps at the base of the box. Fold the side and top pieces around the box, enclosing the gift. Either tie it to close or seal with a sticker.

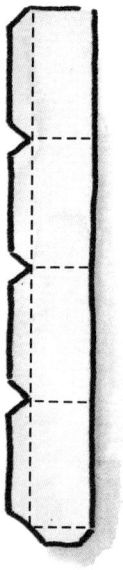

3a To make the red star-shaped box, mark out a strip of card (see 2a), but with the sides of equal measure to form a square box. Make the lid in the same way, but slightly larger.

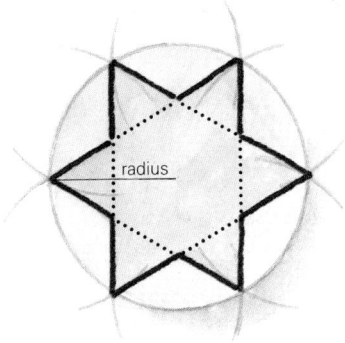

3b To construct the star, measure the length of one side of the box with the compasses. This is the radius of the circle. Draw the circle. Keeping the same radius setting, place the point of the compasses on the circumference of the circle and mark the point it crosses on the curve. Move the compass to this point and repeat the process until you have six points around the circumference. Join alternate points with a pencil and ruler.

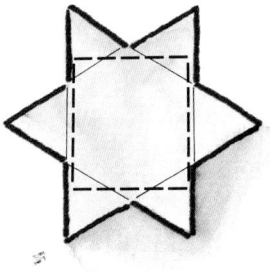

3c Cut out two star shapes and glue one to the flaps at the base of the box and the other to the flaps at the top of the lid. The box is now complete.

Below The possibilities for decorating homemade boxes are endless. Decorated adhesive tape, stickers and attractive ties all add a professional finishing touch. The basket-type box was made using metallic strips of card woven together, see pages 32–3, with a simple strip attached to act as a handle.

COVERING BOXES

Boxes can be re-used; chocolate and soap boxes particularly are often a suitable size for other gifts. There are two ways of disguising their previous uses. Often it is necessary only to re-cover the lid, but the method is the same if the bottom is also being re-covered.

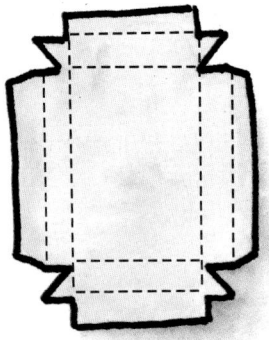

1 Measure the width and length of the box lid and the height of the box sides. The piece of paper will need to be big enough for the lid measurement plus four times the sides. Draw the rectangle in the center of a piece of lightweight paper; add sides all around and then add another set of sides to turn in. Draw "ears" as in the diagram.

2 Cut out, score and fold the whole shape. Position the box on the drawn rectangle, turn the "ears" inward.

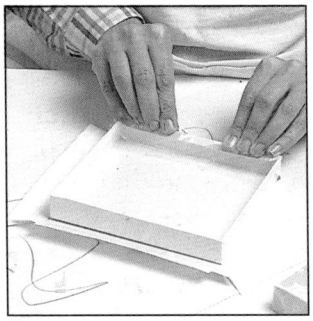

3 Glue the "ears" and the turn-in allowance down.

4 Then glue the opposite sides.

VARIATIONS

Many interesting patterns can be made using corrugated paper; the examples in the photograph (**right**) show two designs. Always cut the corrugated paper with a sharp knife on the wrong (flat) side without pressing hard, because this would flatten the "ribs." Use a fairly strong adhesive. Cover the top first and then, with the covered top downward, wrap a strip of the corrugated paper around the sides.

COMPLEX BOXES

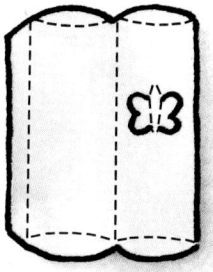

Above Basic plan for the flat gift holder.

FLAT GIFT HOLDER

This type of box is most suitable for flat gifts, such as scarves and ties. Measure the gift and then make the gift holder the length of the gift, and the width plus the height of the gift (if the gift is solid, allow a little extra). At its deepest point, the curves at the top and bottom of the holder should measure approximately twice the height of the gift.

With these measurements it is now possible to draw the plan of the gift holder, see diagram. The curve can either be drawn with the compasses, placed on the center line, or using a dinner plate of suitable size. Join two sides with one curve and trace this off onto a piece of scrap card and use this as a template to draw the other curves. Cut out and score. Stick the glue flap to the side. Place the gift in the holder and close by turning in the curves.

To make the gift holder extra-special, a shape, a butterfly for example, can be cut and folded from the right side; glue a piece of decorative paper underneath and lift the cut-out.

Below The blue gift holder is decorated with a butterfly-shape cut out (see main text). The green holder was made with lightweight card that had been decorated with an abstract stenciled design, see pages 35–7.

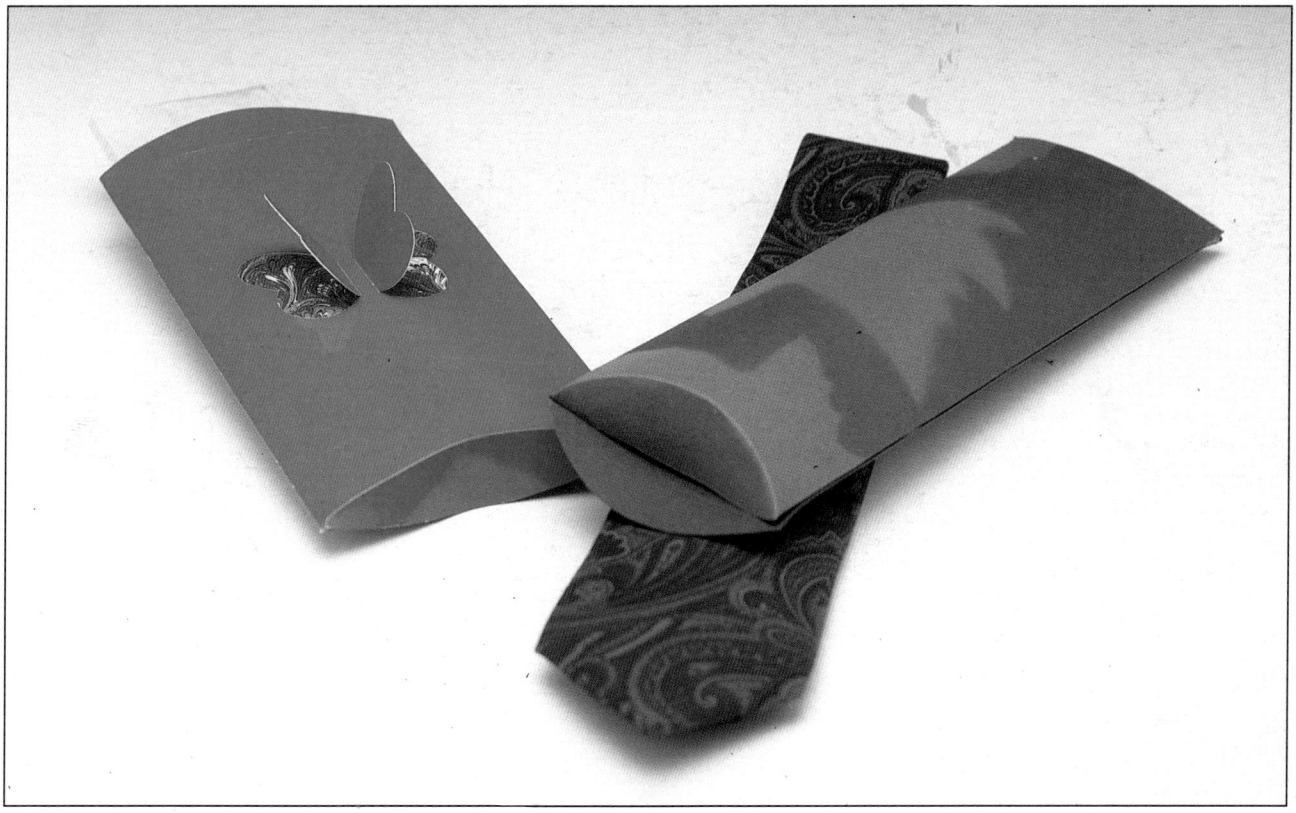

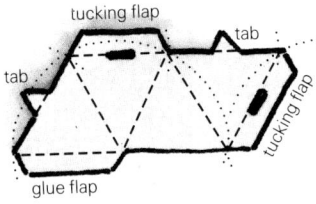

Above Basic plan for the pyramid box.

PYRAMID BOX

This little box can either be used as a box or as a decoration. The size is variable. Start by drawing a line and draw a semicircle on this line. Place the compass point, with the same radius, at one end of the semicircle and mark the center and the point it crosses on the curve. Repeat from the other end. With the same radius setting, draw another semicircle so that it joins the first. Put the compass point on the join and mark the point it crosses on this curve. Join all the marks, and four equilateral triangles will emerge. Add one glue flap to the base of the first triangle, two tucking flaps with slits, and two tabs to correspond with the slits, see diagram. Cut out the basic shape and score all the other lines. Stick the glue flap and place the gift inside and close the box tightly with the tabs – it is quite tricky to tuck in the tabs but ensures a very secure closure.

Below You can make your pyramid box to any size. Use plain or foiled light card, or decorate using the techniques described in the Decorating Paper chapter.

HEXAGONAL BOX

This box looks most impressive and is not as complicated as it appears. Once the size of the hexagon has been worked out it is quite easy to construct. If the box is being used for a circular gift this must fit *within* the hexagon and the correct dimensions should be worked out using scrap paper.

Draw a circle larger than the gift. Draw a horizontal line through the middle of the circle. Using the same radius setting, place the compass point on one of the intersections and mark the point it crosses on the curve. Move the compass to this point and repeat until you have six points around the circumference. Join these points and check whether the gift will fit into this hexagon – if not try again. Once this is correct, draw a plan following the diagram. The sides of the box are equal to the height of the gift and one side of the hexagon in length. The three flaps, top and bottom, are half the height of the hexagon. Cut out, score and fold. Check the angles of the flaps before gluing, in case any adjustments need to be made. Stick the glue flap and assemble the box. If necessary, glue down the tucking flaps on the base so that the box does not fall apart if the gift is heavy.

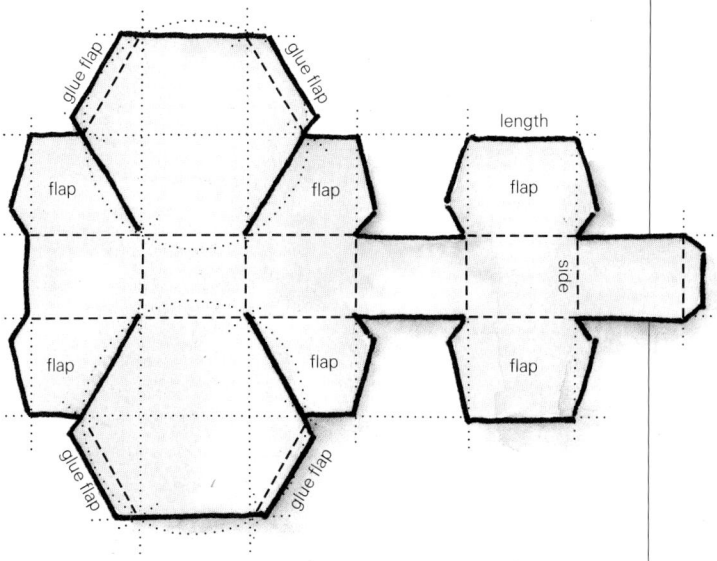

Above The basic plan for the hexagonal box.

Below This hexagonal box has been made using embossed foil card. Filled with chocolates it makes an inexpensive yet impressive gift.

PAPER SHOPPING BAGS

These bags are easy to make and can look extremely decorative. They can be made in many different sizes – tall and thin for bottles, short and wide for cosmetic items – and from many different types of paper. Matching gift tags, see page 92, can be added. Unusual handles can be made from toning or contrasting materials, such as braided wool or ribbons.

Once you have mastered the basic method many variations are possible. Bags can be made in any size using normal gift-wrapping, but the larger the bag the thicker the paper will need to be. It is also possible to use plain paper and decorate it before assembly, see pages 32–50.

There are a few basic rules: all angles should be right angles (90°) so that the bag stands square when finished; the bottom flaps should be approximately ½ in less than the width of the sides; score the fold lines to give a crisper crease; this is essential on thicker paper and card.

BASIC BAG

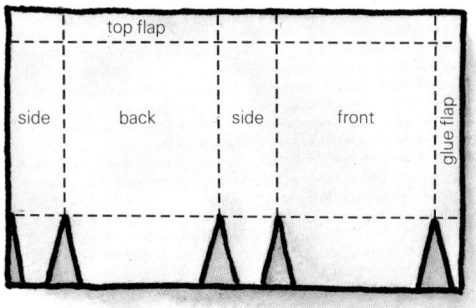

1 It is easiest to work on the wrong side of the paper. Decide on the size of the bag and draw the plan. Cut out the shape, removing the shaded areas. Score the dotted lines lightly, and fold and then unfold them.

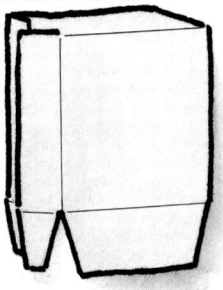

2 Glue down the top flap, which adds strength and looks neater. Next glue the front flap to the side.

3 Finally, glue the bottom flaps to each other – the side flaps to the back flap and the front flap on top of the side flaps.

Left For the handles, punch holes in the top edge and thread ribbons, cord or braid through them. The holes can act as closures or can be simply decorative.

STRONG PAPER BAG

Making a bag which will carry a bottle or a heavy or large gift poses a few problems, but these can easily be overcome. If a bottle or heavy gift is to be placed in the bag, it is advisable to glue a piece of card inside the base of the bag. To strengthen the top of the bag, add an extra strip of paper under the top flap. The basic plan is the same as for the ordinary bag, page 84, except that the measurements for all the sides will be identical and should be the diameter of the bottle plus ¼ in. The height of the bag should be 2½ in more than the height of the bottle, so that the top edges can be drawn together.

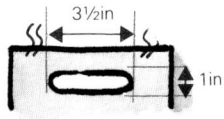

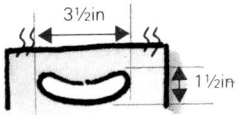

1 When making a large bag it is quite simple to add a strong handle. Cut a piece of plain lightweight card the width of the bag and at least 3 in deep. Cut the hand shape out of the center of the card and mark this hole on the bag plan. Cut these holes out of the paper on the bag and top flap, and glue the card stiffener in position. Continue as for the basic bag.

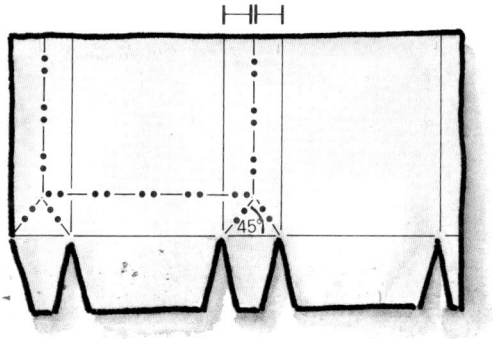

2 It is possible to fold the bag flat by scoring lines in addition to the ones on the basic plan. Practice with some scrap paper – this is not as complicated as it looks.

HEART-SHAPED BAG

The decorative heart-shaped bag shown on this page is deceptively simple. The design is based on a semicircle and can be made from many different types of paper or card. It is easy to alter the size by following the directions.

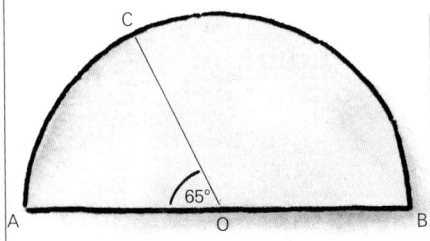

1 Draw a semicircle and mark a point about 65° from one edge, at C.

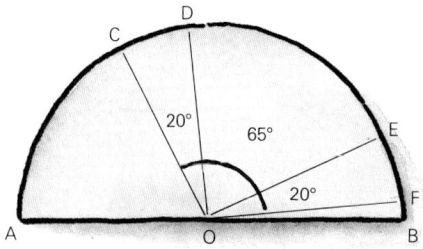

2 Mark another point 20° from C, then another at 65° and another at 20°. Join all these points to the center.

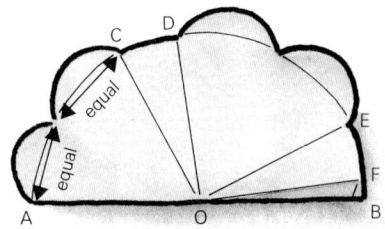

3 Now divide both of the largest arcs in half, either by measuring or using a protractor. Draw semicircles on each half.

Below Punch holes in the side panels and make handles. Decorate the bag if you wish. For inspiration see pages 32–50.

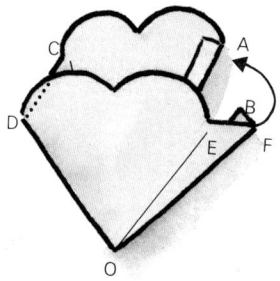

4 Cut out the whole shape and score all lines from the center out to the edge and fold. Glue the shaded area to the heart shape.

WRAPPING IDEAS

The art of wrapping and the art of giving could be said to be one and the same. A beautifully wrapped box shows that you have chosen and wrapped a gift with care.

The ideas in this chapter offer a basic introduction to the art of wrapping. The secret is to choose your wrapping papers with care, then to fold them neatly. Accessories such as ribbons, bows or gift tags are important decorative features which help to personalize a gift, but they will not disguise a badly wrapped box.

Almost any paper can be used to wrap a gift. Conventional, patterned gift-wrap papers are good, but consider using more unusual papers such as tissue paper, Ingres (Strathmore) paper and other papers from artists' supply stores and stationers. In particular, consider using decorated papers, see pages 32–50. A hand-decorated wrapping paper will give your gift a special personal touch that will have great meaning for the receiver. Some decorating techniques, such as folding and dipping, see pages 42–5, are best done with paper that is too thin to use as wrapping, so back them with another sheet for extra strength.

THE PERFECT WRAP

This is the best way to wrap a box so that it looks neat and well folded. The method will work for a box of any shape.

1 Place the gift box on the wrapping paper. Trim the long edges of the sheet so that the overlap at the sides is the same as the height of the box. Fold over a hem of 1 in along one short edge.

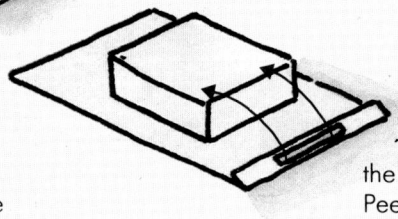

2 Fix a strip of double-sided adhesive tape to the hem, almost the length of the box. Peel off the backing, then stick the hem to the top of the box 2 in beyond the nearside edge.

3 Trim the other short side of the wrapping paper to length, so that when a 1-in hem is folded over and a strip of double-sided adhesive tape attached, the edge will fold up and stick to the box, level with the furthest edge.

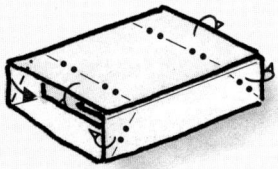

4 Push in the sheet as shown. Be careful to keep it neat.

5 Fold in side triangles to lie flat against the box, forming a tapered point at the bottom.

6 Stick a small piece of double-sided adhesive tape on the tapered point and fold up.

7 The box complete. Reinforce all the creases as the finishing touch.

PLEATED WRAPS

Here are three simple ways to pleat a sheet of wrapping paper to hold a name tag, a sheet of complemen tary wrapping paper or a decorative form. As ever, be careful to fold as neatly as possible, perhaps practicing on scrap paper first.

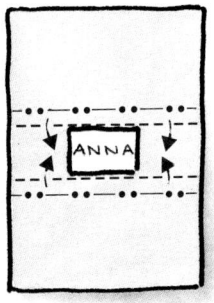

1a For each, first make your item to be inserted between the pleats, preferably from thick paper or card. It can be any size, but the larger it is the farther apart the pleats will be. Place the card in the middle of the wrapping paper.

1b Carefully construct two pleats across the top and bottom of the inserted card so that the top pleat folds downward and the bottom one folds upward, trapping it between the pleats. The depth of the pleats should be at least ¾ in.

1c Continue to wrap as described in "The Perfect Wrap" above. This will create a wrapped gift with pleats running down the length of the box.

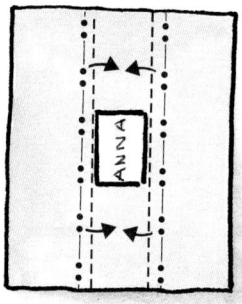

2a Here the pleats run along the length of the wrap, so that in the finished wrap they lie across the box.

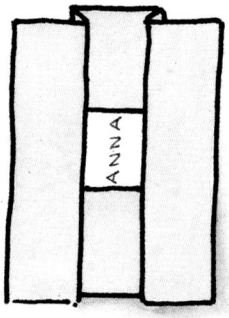

2b Construct the pleats and fold over the card as before.

2c The wrap complete.

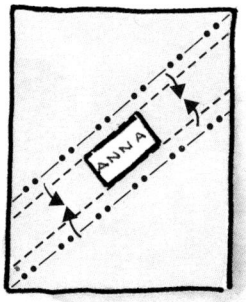

3a An unusual variation. Lay the card at an angle in the middle of the wrapping paper and form the pleats as before.

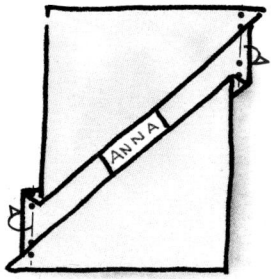

3b Fold the excess paper behind (or cut it off), to restore the rectangular shape of the sheet.

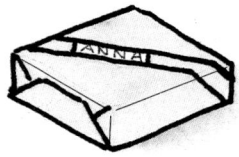

3c Wrap as before to create a band of pleats set at an angle to the sides of the box.

TIPS

Try experimenting with other patterns of pleats to create practical or decorative features on a gift-wrapped box: horizontal pleats crossing vertical pleats; pleats across a corner; lines of parallel pleats and so on. The effects can be surprisingly creative.

ANNA-

RIBBONS AND BOWS

RIBBONS

Ribbons are excellent ways to turn a plainly wrapped box into an attractively wrapped gift. Not all gift boxes need ribbons though – those that are wrapped in elaborately patterned gift-wrap paper may well be attractive enough as they are, or perhaps with an additional bow or gift tag.

Long lengths of gift-wrap ribbon can be purchased in many gift shops or card stores. Exciting and unconventional ribbons can be found in the fabric departments of stores. These range from hair ribbons to lace edging. Homemade ribbons can be made using strips cut from large sheets of paper decorated using the techniques described on pages 32–50. Alternatively, braided wools make pretty ribbons.

An interesting use of ribbon is to braid or weave together two or more colors. The "under-and-over" pattern can vary and the ribbons can either be set square onto the box or set at an angle. See below for further ideas. Be careful not to cover too much of the gift with ribbons, or it may look over-decorated.

BOWS

Intricate bows already made up can often be purchased from gift shops or card stores, particularly in the weeks before Christmas. They are awkward to make well at home, requiring the construction of wooden templates and a lot of practice.

Here, though, is a simple but very attractive bow, sometimes called "My Lady." It works equally well made from gift-wrap ribbon, fabric ribbon or paper strips.

1 Cut a length of ribbon about 22 in long and twist it as shown, being careful to make both loops the same size. Secure the center with a staple.

2 Cut another length of ribbon about 13 in long and form three loops as shown, beginning with the middle one. Trim off any excess. Check that it will fit between the loops of the other piece of ribbon.

3 Staple the second piece of ribbon to the first, being careful to line up all the layers and to center the second piece on top. To complete the bow, cut a V-shaped notch into the ends of the ribbon.

GIFT TAGS

Gift tags are one of the finishing touches of a present and a little imagination can make even this small piece of paper quite special. They can be quick and easy to make or quite intricate.

Gift tags can be single or double. They can be attached with a punched hole and cord or stuck directly onto the packages. There are many types of cord available in the shops with which to attach the tag – ribbons, wool, or metallic string – or braid together threads to match the colors of the gift wrap.

Use card cut to the required size or shape, scored and folded, if making a double card. If you use paper, it may be necessary to glue this to another piece of paper so that it is not too floppy. This method could also be used to make a card from the paper used to wrap the gift.

Plain tags can be decorated with stickers, quilled shapes (see below) and miniature origami.

QUILLS

EQUIPMENT

- Strips of paper
- Glue
- Toothpicks, matchsticks or dowel rod
- Scissors – optional
- Tweezers – optional
- Waxed paper

Quilling uses rolled strips of paper to form shapes, which can be glued together to make patterns. The designs can then be used in numerous ways, for example, glued on cards for gift tags or greeting cards, as decorations for boxes, as mobiles or stencils. Quilling is sometimes known as paper filigree and was used by monks in the 15th century to make panels of imitation gold filigree. In the Victorian period quilling was considered a very ladylike pursuit and tea-caddies were a popular item for decoration.

Traditionally the strips are ⅛ in wide and the length can vary. The strips can sometimes be bought in stationery shops or can be laboriously cut by hand, or party streamers can be used – these are usually a little wider, but the principle remains the same.

Using a toothpick, matchstick or thin dowel rod with a split, place one end of the strip in the split and turn it slowly and evenly so that the strip remains level. When the paper is completely rolled, squeeze it lightly to make a tight curve before removing the stick. This coil is a loose open coil.

BASIC COILS

Loose open coil.

Loose coil with the end glued down. Most shapes are made from the loose coil.

Tight coil – the end is glued before removing from the stick.

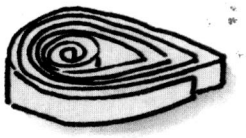

Pear drop – squeeze the side that has been stuck, to a point.

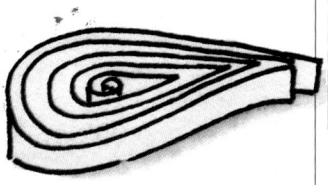

Petal – as pear drop but curved gently at the same time as squeezing to form the point.

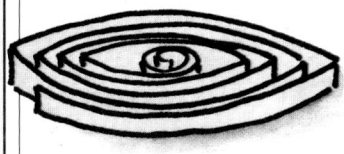

Eye-shape – both ends are pointed and the whole shape is elongated slightly.

Leaf-shape – as eye-shape but curved gently in both directions.

DECORATING WITH QUILLS

Patterns can be planned in advance or built up as you go along. In either case, it is best to work on a piece of waxed paper so that the design can be moved around as the work progresses, without getting stuck. This is especially important if the piece is to be used on its own. If the design is being made as a decoration for an object, it can be worked directly onto the object by glueing the center of the shape and placing each part carefully in position. Tweezers or an extra toothpick will be useful. Finished designs can be sprayed with paint or varnish.

V-shape – creased at the halfway point and rolled outward.

Heart-shape – as V-shape but rolled inward.

Triangle – squeezed in three places.

S-shape – rolled in opposite directions from both ends.

Scroll-shape – rolled in the same direction from both ends.

TWIST-OUTS, CUT-AWAYS AND POP-UPS

EQUIPMENT

- Card
- A scalpel or craft knife
- Something to cut on
- A pair of scissors
- A pencil and a ruler

These three similar techniques are exciting ways to create imaginative three-dimensional greeting cards or decorations. They are all simple to make, but will be best understood if you first follow the instructions that explain how to produce a basic example of each technique.

TWIST-OUTS

Twist-outs are particularly ingenious ways to create three-dimensional cards, suspended decorations or simply beautiful shapes to be admired. Use thin card for finished examples – paper is too weak and thick card too cumbersome to bend easily.

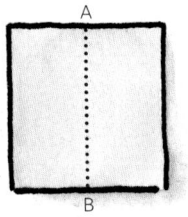

1 For the basic method, draw line AB down the center of a piece of scrap card or paper.

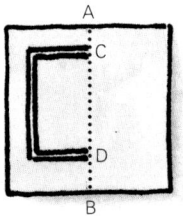

2 With a blade, incise line C to D, so that the incision starts and ends on AB. (Note that AC is shorter than DB.)

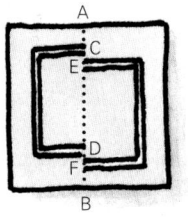

3 Next, incise line E to F, so that the incision once again starts and ends on AB. Note that E is below C and F is below D.

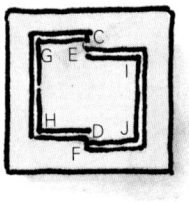

4 Pull edge GH toward you and push IJ away from you, forming short creases between CE and DF.

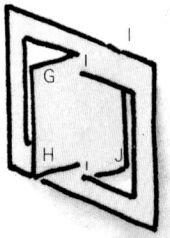

5 The center of the card will twist out from its frame.

Below right This technique, once mastered, will produce decorations and sculptural forms of great beauty. Study the examples in the photograph, then experiment with your own ideas.

VARIATIONS

The following are variations of the basic technique. The principle is that line AB can be anywhere on a sheet of card. The incisions can be any shape, but they must begin and end on AB, so that CE and DF can be creased along one uninterrupted line.

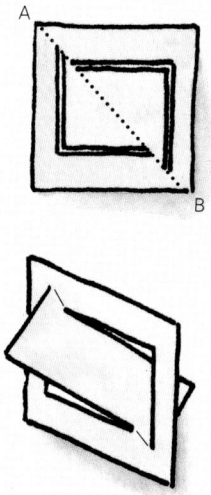

Draw AB along a diagonal, so that when incisions are made, the center twists out from its frame along a diagonal axis.

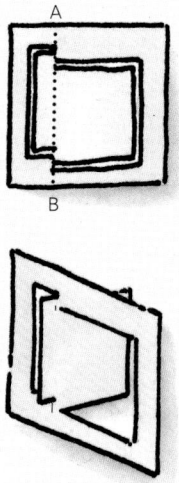

Draw AB toward the lefthand edge, so that the center twists out a long way on the right but very little on the left.

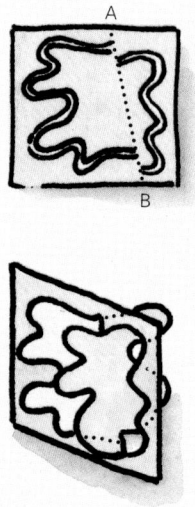

Draw AB in an arbitrary position and doodle incisions on it at random.

GREETING CARDS

Here are three twist-outs in the form of greeting cards. The letters could be reworked to say HAPPY BIRTHDAY, GET WELL, GOOD LUCK, etc.

Other good festive themes include candles, stars, baubles or stockings.

If you draw AB on the horizontal, this creates possibilities for sculptural cards on a wide variety of themes, including all those suggested above. Remember, any shape – no matter how unlikely – can be made to twist out. Invent your own to suit an occasion that requires you to send a card.

Below left Twist-outs make highly individual greeting cards. The wording and shapes can be altered to suit every occasion.

Below right Concentric twist-outs make fascinating mobiles. Simply thread a strong piece of thread through the middle of the outer frame.

CONCENTRIC DESIGNS

Once you have understood and practiced the basic twist-out technique, try making concentric incisions.

GRAND COUNTY PUBLIC LIBRARY
25 SOUTH 1st EAST
MOAB, UTAH 84532

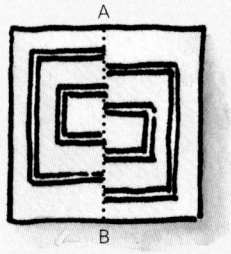

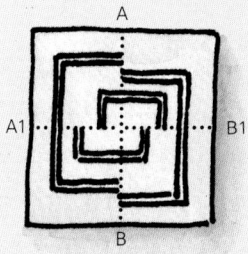

The simplest way of doing this is to retain AB as the single line along which all incisions start and end. Cut all the incisions, then twist out each alternate frame, working towards the centre.

An intriguing elaboration is to introduce a second line (A_1B_1) on which to start and end incisions. Whereas the previous design creates vertical frames, this will also produce horizontal ones. Other lines (A_2B_2, A_3B_3 etc.) may be introduced to make concentric shapes twist out at many different angles.

GRAND COUNTY PUBLIC LIBRARY
25 SOUTH 1st EAST
MOAB, UTAH 84532

CUT-AWAYS

This easy technique is an interesting way to make a shape of card project beyond a crease, creating an unusual silhouette. It looks particularly good when used on a greeting card. Use card of thin to medium thickness.

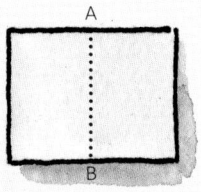

BASIC METHOD

1 Draw line AB down the middle.

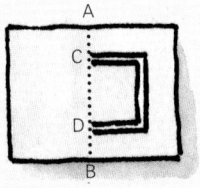

2 With a blade, incise line C to D starting and ending on AB.

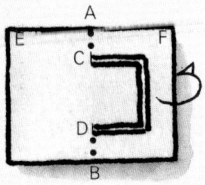

3 Make a mountain crease between AC and DB, so that corner F bends backward to touch E. Do not crease between C and D.

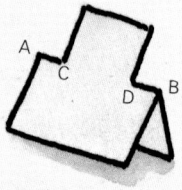

4 The card should look like this, with a rectangle of card projecting beyond the crease.

VARIATIONS

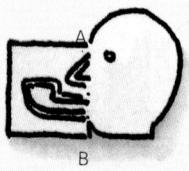

You could make a cut-away nose and pipe, with the outline of the other half of the card cut to the profile of a head.

Here the card beyond the heart has been lost to one side of crease AB.

When the top half of the numerals project beyond the crease, the card beyond the bottom half of the numerals can be cut away to complete their silhouettes.

POP-UPS

Of the three techniques explained in this chapter, pop-ups can become the most technical. This section shows how versatile the simpler pop-up techniques are. If you wish to see more complex examples, look at some of the remarkably clever pop-up books in the children's section of a good bookshop. Pop-ups can be used in combination with the cut-away techniques explained in the previous section, helping to break the symmetry of a pop-up shape. Use thin card, but practice on stiff paper.

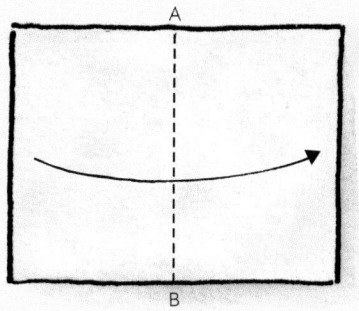

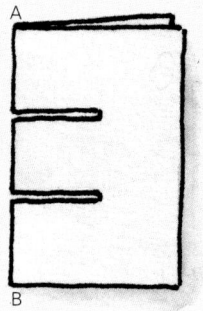

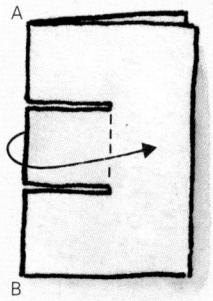

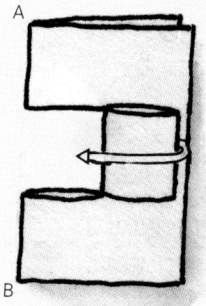

BASIC METHOD
1 Crease a piece of card along AB and fold the card in half along the crease.

2 With a pair of scissors, make two cuts from crease AB almost halfway across the sheet.

3 Fold the section between the cuts over to the right, pulling it over as far as it will go, connecting the ends of the cuts with a crease.

4 Unfold the center section.

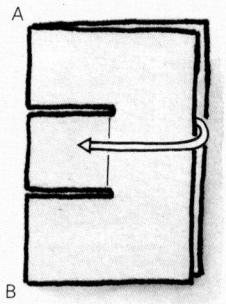

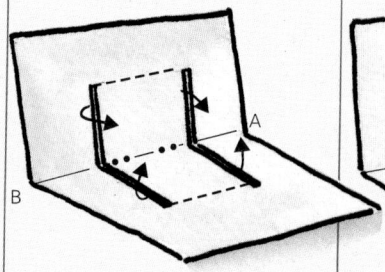

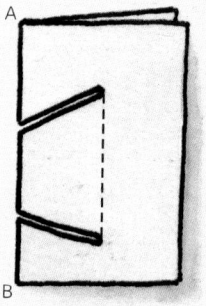

5 Open the sheet.

6 Do not flatten the sheet, but keep a valley crease along AB.

7 Lift up the thin belt of card between the cuts, so that the valley crease down the middle of the belt pops up and becomes a mountain crease.

VARIATIONS A The cuts do not have to be perpendicular to crease AB, as step 2. They can be angled as shown here.

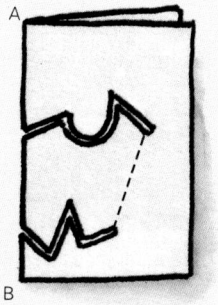

B The crease made in step 3 need not be parallel to AB – it can be at any angle. The cuts can also be any shape.

C To make a "second-generation pop-up," follow steps 1 to 7 of the basic method. Fold the pop-up flat and make two cuts only into the nearside crease (**right**), then proceed as in steps 2 to 7. The second-generation pop-up complete (**far right**). By repeating this process a third generation, then a fourth, etc., can be made to pop up.

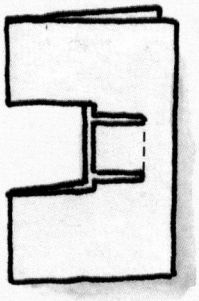

MULTI POP-UPS

The pop-ups made so far have all been built up from a central crease AB (see step 1). However, by starting with more than one crease, you can make decorations that are fully three-dimensional. Here is one suggestion.

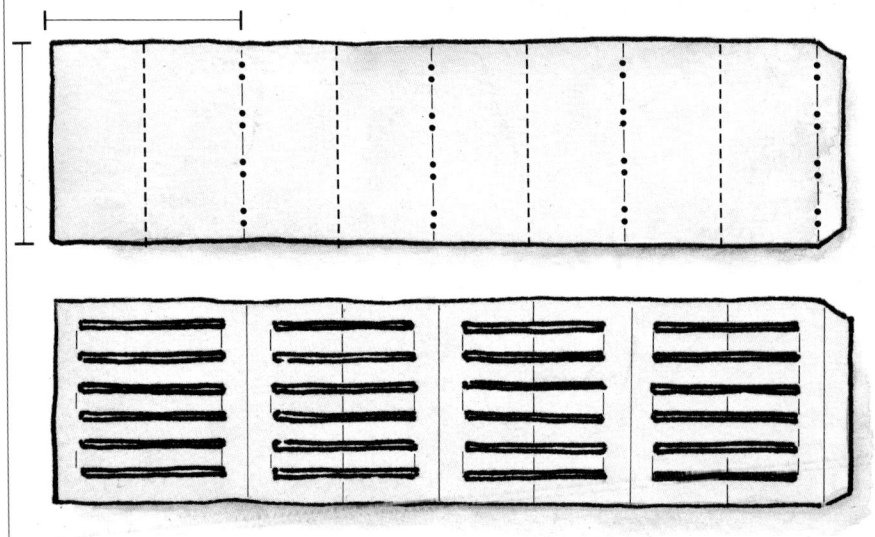

1 Cut out a piece of thin card four times as long as it is high, with a small tab on the end for glueing. Pleat it into eighths, alternating the mountain and valley creases.

2 Make 24 cuts as shown.

3 Pleat the strip and glue the tab to hold the pleats in the shape of a cross. Pull out the belts of card between the cuts.

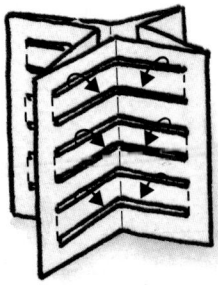

Above right Suggestions for pop-up cards are illustrated here. Some are first-generation pop-ups, some have two o more generations, and others have incorporated cut-away techniques.

Right The cross-shape opened out, with suggested variations.

STATIONERY

CARD FOLDS AND IDEAS

Fig 1

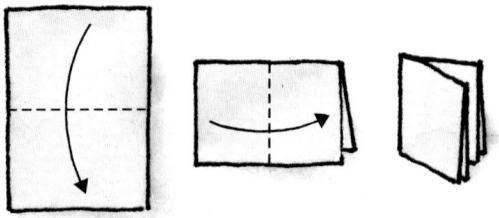

Fig 2

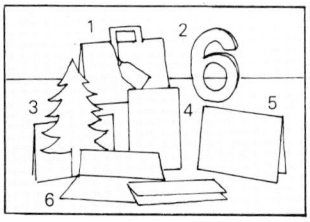

Left These cards are all made from the basic folds shown above: 1 and 2 are designs cut from a single fold (see Fig 1); 3 is a single fold with a cut-out shape glued on; 4 is a double fold (see Fig 2) with a paper weaving decoration attached to the face; 5 is a single fold decorated with a collage made of adhesive-backed paper; 6 is a single fold card with a basic envelope, see page 106.

BASIC CARD FOLDS

There are many ways to fold a piece of card or paper to form the basis of a greeting card. Some are simple and well known, whereas others are a little more complicated. The illustrations here show some basic starting points and the photographs indicate how they can be made into attractive greeting cards. Use thin card, except for Figs 2, 6 and 7, for which thicker paper is best. See page 8 for a guide to paper and card weights.

The techniques shown in other chapters of the book can be adapted to form cards, especially those in Decorating Paper (pages 32–50), Origami (pages 58–74) and Twist-outs, Cut-aways and Pop-ups (pages 96–102). Think of the type of card fold and paper technique that best suit the occasion – the variations are endless.

ADDITIONAL FOLDS

Fig 3

Fig 4

Fig 5

Fig 6

Fig 7

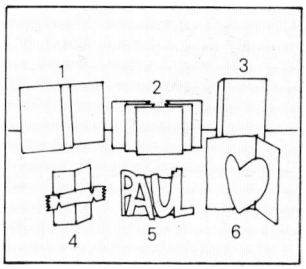

Left Most of these cards are made from folds shown above: 1 is made from the fold in Fig 6; 2 is made from the fold shown in Fig 7 and decorated with purchased stickers; 3 is made from the fold in Fig 4 – the righthand flap has been cut out to act as a mount for the photograph; 4 and 5 are made from the fold in Fig 5 and are both cut-outs; 6 is made from the fold in Fig 2 using the pop-up technique explained on page 101.

BASIC ENVELOPE

Having practiced some of the techniques in the previous chapters, it will no longer be necessary for you to buy greeting cards or even an envelope to fit any card, because you will be able to make your own. It is also easy to decorate stationery and to make a holder as a really unusual gift.

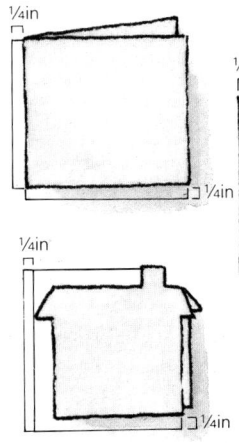

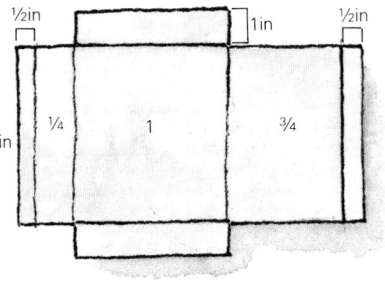

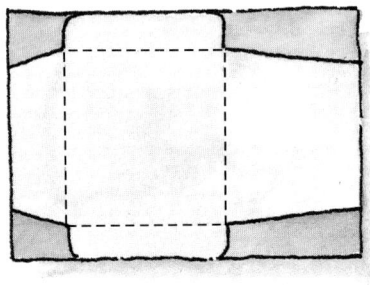

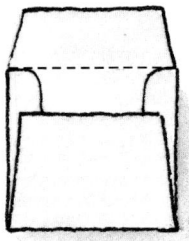

1 Measure the card and add ¼ in to the length and the width (**top**). If the card is an irregular shape (**above**) add extra to the widest points.

2 Plan the size of paper required for the envelope: the side flaps should be at least 1 in; the bottom flap should be three-quarters the width of the card plus ½ in for closing; and the top flap should be a quarter the width plus ½ in.

3 Draw this shape on your chosen paper and cut it out. (Use a coin to draw the curves of the slide flaps.) Taper the top and bottom flaps. Score the dotted lines.

4 Turn in the side flaps. Apply glue to the side edges of the bottom flap, turn it up and stick it to the side flaps. The envelope is now ready to be used. To close the envelope, either use glue or double-sided adhesive tape along the top flap.

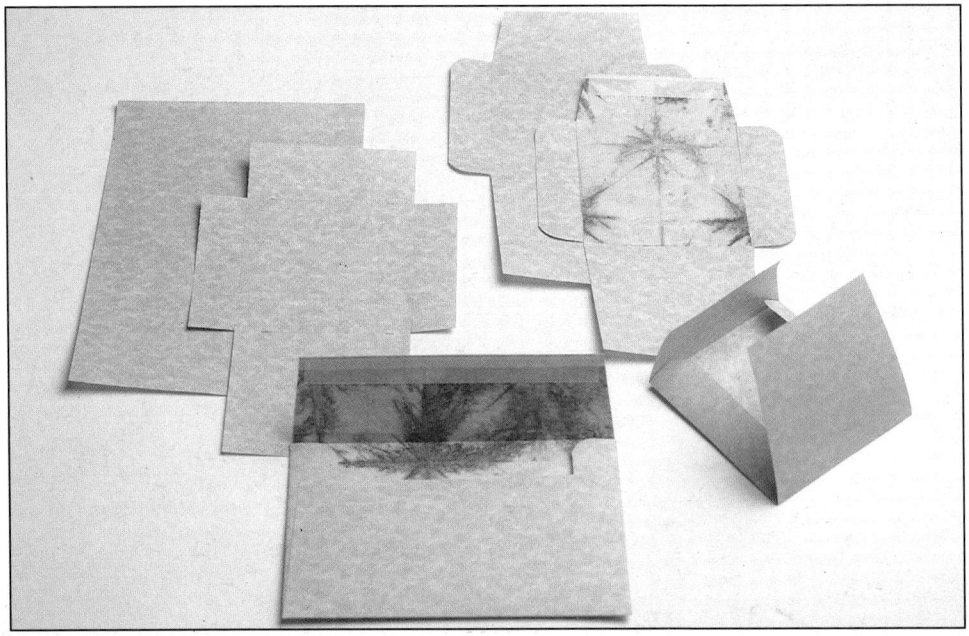

Left You could line the basic envelope using plain colored tissue paper or folded and dyed paper, see pages 42–5. Add the lining before you turn in the side flaps. Cut a piece of lining paper the width of the envelope and the length of the envelope minus the bottom flap. Glue it in position before assembling the envelope.

Right The envelopes in the photograph have been folded from a piece of paper the same size as the pieces on which they are lying.

FOLDED ENVELOPE 1

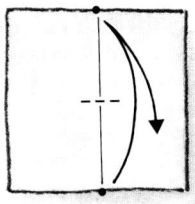

1 Begin with a square of paper, creased vertically down the middle. Fold the bottom edge up to the top and press it flat in the middle to find the mid-point of the square.

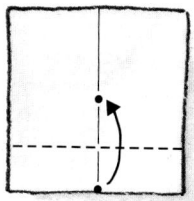

2 Fold the bottom edge up to the center.

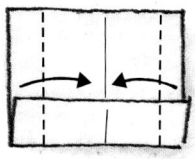

3 Fold in the sides, as shown.

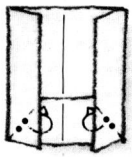

4 Fold the loose corners behind at the bottom.

5 Fold the top corners into the center vertical crease.

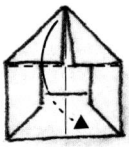

6 Crease across the base of the top triangles, tucking them inside the pocket. This locks the envelope shut.

7 The complete envelope. Write the address on the side without any folds.

FOLDED ENVELOPE 2

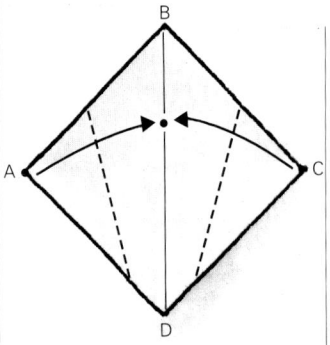

1 Using a square piece of paper, crease a diagonal line BD and unfold it. Fold corners A and C onto the crease, so that the new creases made do not quite run down to corner D.

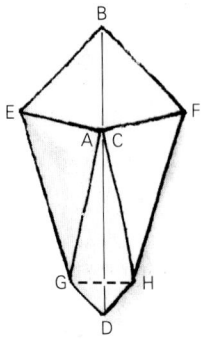

2 Crease and unfold G to H.

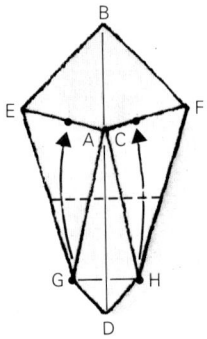

3 Fold up D so that corner G lies on edge EA and corner H on CF.

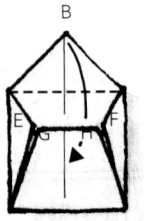

5 Slide B under edge GH and push it until it will not go any further. Flatten and crease.

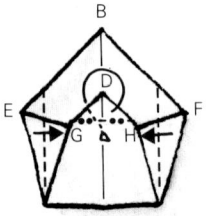

4 Fold D inside, tucking it behind A and C; this locks G and H flat. Fold in E and F, butting them hard against the edges that run up to G and H.

6 The complete envelope. To unlock it, pull out corner B.

Left Again, the envelopes in the photograph have been folded from a piece of paper the same size as the pieces on which they are lying.

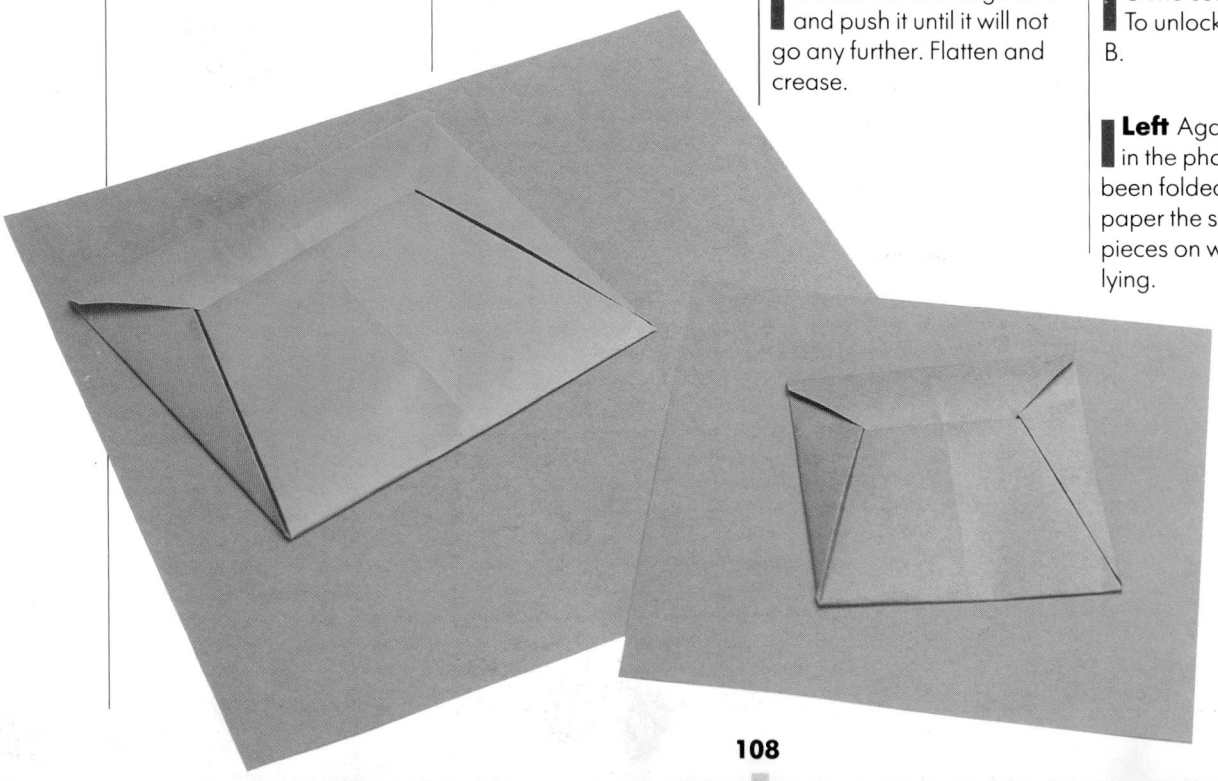

STATIONERY HOLDER

EQUIPMENT

- Board 1/16 in thick
- Covering and lining material
- Starch-filled buckram (see page 112)
- Pencil, ruler, compass or dividers
- Knife and scissors
- Glue
- Bone folder
- Newsprint or computer paper for scrap paper

This design can be made to take most sizes of writing paper and notecards.

Measure the stationery and add 3/4 in to the length and the width; these two measurements will determine the size of the boards. Cut two boards to size, making sure that the corners are square and that the grain runs from top to bottom, see page 9. To allow for turn-ins, covering materials should overlap all edges by 1/2 in, unless otherwise stated. Lining materials should be 1/2 in smaller than the overall measurements of the board.

Draw a line down one side of the board one-fifth of the overall width. Mark this with a pair of compasses or dividers and also mark the corner on the diagonal. Repeat for the other board. (See Fig 1.)

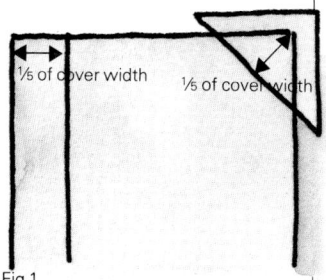

Fig 1

1 Cut the buckram to size – twice as wide as the marked line plus at least 3/4 in to accommodate the contents, and as long as the boards plus turn-ins. Cut a lining piece – remember constants.

2 To cut the buckram for the corners place a scrap of paper along the marked line and add 1/2 in to overlap the edges, see Fig 1. Measure the square edges and cut two squares of buckram. Cut across them diagonally to make triangles to cover the corners.

3 Brush glue onto the wrong side of the buckram cut for the spine – the glue should be the consistency of thick cream. Using a firm brush and scrap paper, work the glue from the center of the piece out toward and over the edges onto the scrap paper.

4 Position the spine on the boards between the marked lines and turn over the edges using a bone folder or clean fingers.

5 Glue the lining strip in position and, using the bone folder, press the buckram well to form a groove; start from one side and work across.

6 Mark the position of one of the triangular pieces of buckram and trim off the corner.

7 Glue the piece into position on the diagonal line and press it toward the corner. Turn over and, using the bone folder, press the edge down and work the miter neatly into boards. Finally bring the second edge over and press it down. Repeat for the other three corners.

8 Now, mark the covering material, remembering to add extra for the turn-ins on the edges and slightly overlapping the buckram at the spine. Position the covering material on the board and, holding it down firmly, fold back one corner so that it just covers the buckram triangle, and crease. Repeat for the other corner. Remove from the board and trim away the corners at the folded crease.

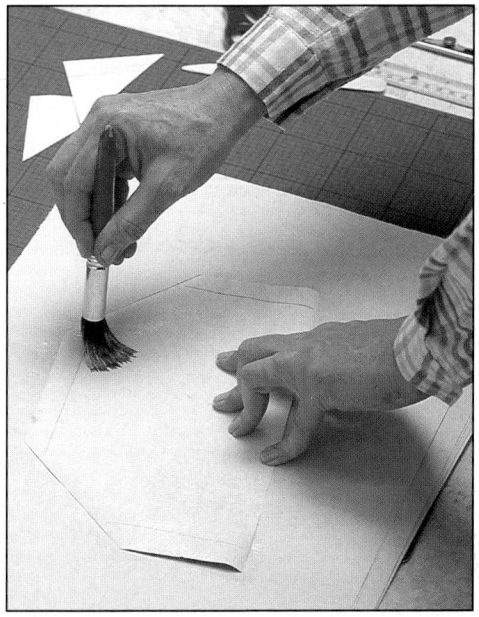

9 Before gluing mark the position of the turn-ins on the wrong side.

10 Work quickly, because the covering material may curl when moistened with glue.

11 Place the glued piece on the board and cover it with a piece of scrap paper. Smooth it over gently with the bone folder to remove any air bubbles. The scrap paper protects the covering material from becoming shiny with rubbing.

12 Now turn in the edges neatly, adding more glue if necessary.

13 If you want ribbon ties attach them at this stage. Cut two lengths of about 12 in. Using a knife or chisel, cut a hole the width of the ribbon in the center of both boards ½ in from the side edge.

14 Push the ribbons through these holes and glue them in place. Cover the right side with a scrap of board and hammer it to close and flatten the incision (this step is not essential).

ALTERNATIVES

Buckram is usually available from specialist stores selling bookbinding materials – check your local suppliers. An alternative to buckram is to laminate lightweight canvas or sturdy cloth (sailcloth is ideal) to paper. Brush a thin layer of glue onto lightweight paper and smooth the paper carefully onto the cloth. Cover it with scrap paper and smooth it gently all over with a bone folder or the side of your hand to remove the air bubbles. Allow it to dry under weights – a pile of books or something similar.

LINING

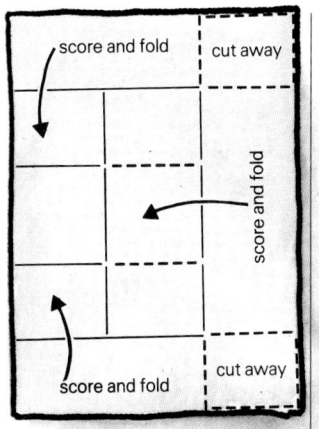

Fig 2

1 Position the lefthand lining on the righthand lining paper so that the lefthand edges are together and the excess equal at top and bottom. Using the lefthand lining as a guide, score the righthand lining paper right across the top and bottom and down the side. Trim away the top and bottom righthand rectangles. Score a second line ¼ in from the previous scores toward the outside edge of all three flaps. Crease and fold in – the paper now appears the same size as the board minus the lining constants, and is ready to glue into position.

To line the folder there is a variety of possibilities: you could line the righthand board with plain paper with flaps to protect the contents of the holder and to stop them falling out; you could line the lefthand board quite simply with a piece of plain paper glued in place or it could have a pocket attached for envelopes; the pocket could be made of decorative paper or it could be a different shape – see the photograph of the finished project.

For the righthand lining, cut a piece of paper 1½ times as wide and 1½ times as long as the boards, with the grain running from top to bottom, see Fig 2. For the lefthand lining, cut one piece the same size as the boards, less the constants for lining. For the pocket, cut one piece half the length of the board and the full width plus 1 in.

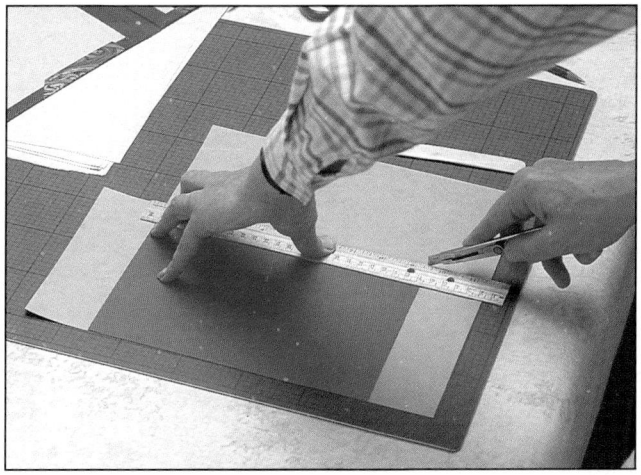

2 Score the paper cut for the pocket, using a ruler and a bone folder, ½ in in from the top and bottom edges. Fold and glue down one edge. This is to strengthen the top edge of the pocket. Place the pocket on the lefthand lining paper so that it overlaps equally at both sides. Score and fold in these edges.

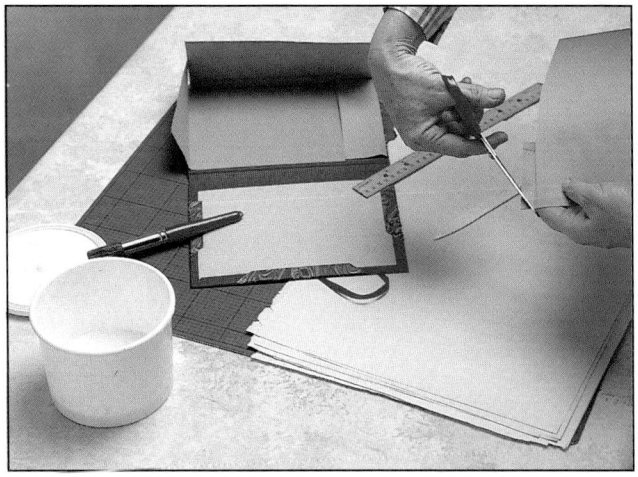

3 Trim away the double fold of the pocket as a miter to reduce bulk. Taper, very slightly, the lower side edges of the lining for the same reason.

4 Glue the folded flaps of the pocket to the lining paper. Then glue the whole piece into position on the lefthand board.

TABLE DECORATIONS

NAPKIN FOLDS

The use of paper as a means of table decoration is often forgotten. Most people take paper and its many uses for granted and, although paper napkins are used each day, it is seldom that one thinks of folding them decoratively or of using a little imagination to make simple place cards or napkin rings. Using the ideas found in this chapter, it is easy to draw together the whole table setting. Make a theme for the whole setting by choosing a color, perhaps picked out from the dinner service or tablecloth, or use a topic to suit the season.

SAIL NAPKIN

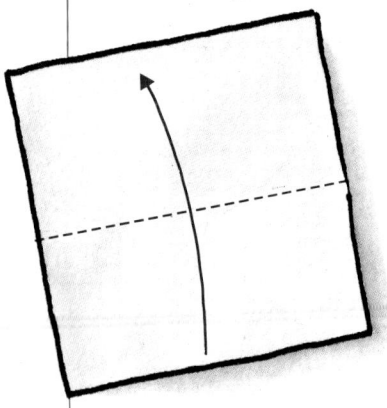

1 Fold the bottom edge up to the top.

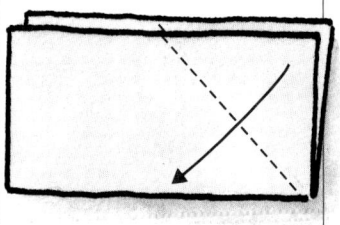

2 Fold down the top righthand corner.

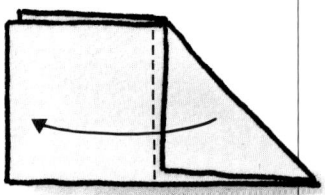

3 Fold the bottom right corner across to the left edge.

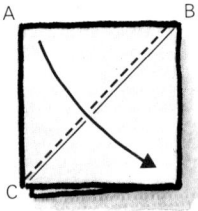

4 Fold corner A downward. Note B and C.

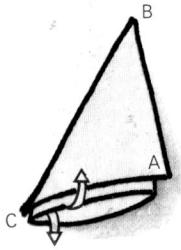

5 Open corner C, flattening the crease BC.

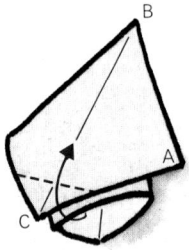

6 Fold up the tip of corner C . . .

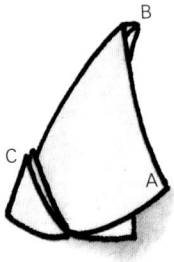

7 . . . to lock and complete the sail napkin.

Right This is a simple, attractive napkin, quick to make and easy to unfold.

FLAME NAPKIN

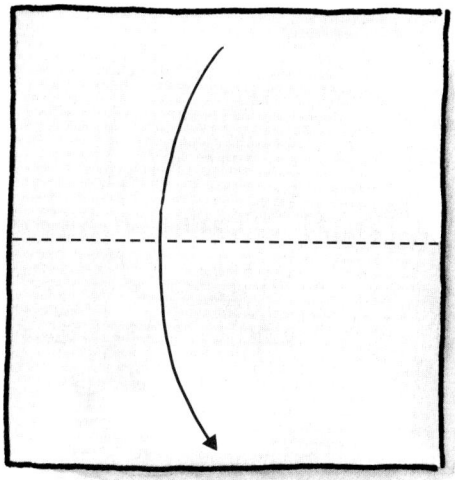

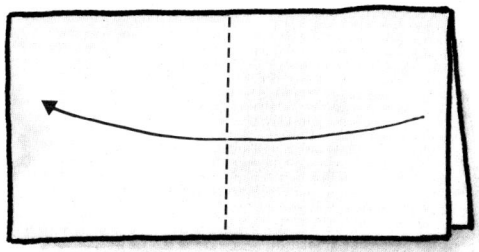

1 Fold the top edge down to the bottom.

2 Fold the righthand edge over to the left.

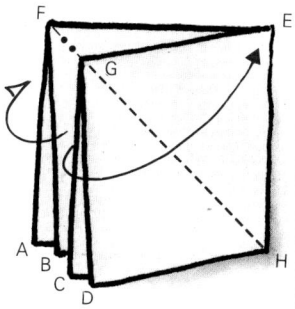

3 Look carefully at the lettered corners. Fold A and B behind to touch E and fold C and D to the front to also touch E. Crease FH and GH . . .

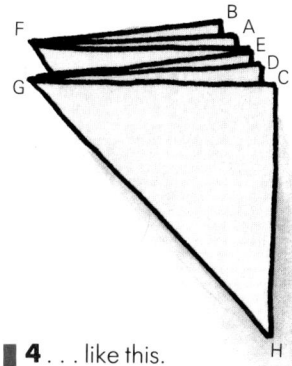

4 . . . like this.

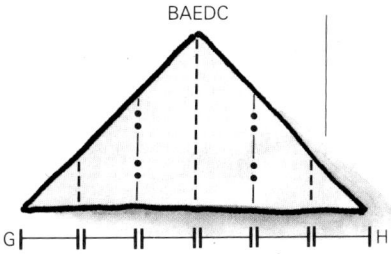

5 Pleat the triangle into six equal divisions, to look . . .

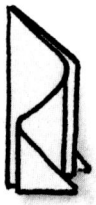

6 . . . like this.

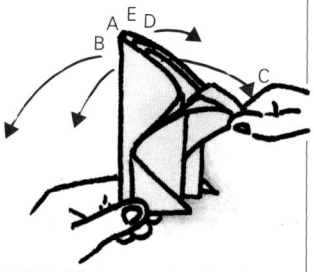

7 Hold the napkin firmly at the bottom. There are five layers of corners at the top. Tug corner C as shown, pulling it as far out as possible. Do the same with corner D next to it, but not pulling it as far. Repeat on the other side, pulling B further than A.

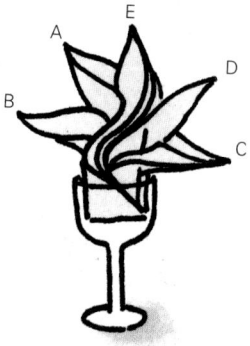

8 The flame napkin is complete. To hold its shape, the design needs to be placed in a wine glass or tumbler.

Left This fold is more complex than the previous one, but makes a spectacular display. Fold two together of different colors for extra visual effect.

NAPKIN RING

EQUIPMENT

- Paper or card
- Materials to decorate the paper
- Card for template
- Pencil
- Ruler
- Knife or a pair of scissors

A good size for the ring is 6 in by 1 in plus ½ in at each end for the slit, which will be cut halfway at each end – see Fig 1. It is quite important that the grain of the paper runs in the direction of the arrow, so that it will curve easily. If you are making a curved center (see Fig 2) it is advisable to make a template of the shape from card (see Fig 3) – this saves you drawing each one separately.

Having drawn the shape, cut it out using a knife or scissors, slide the slits together and pass the napkin through the ring, see Fig 4.

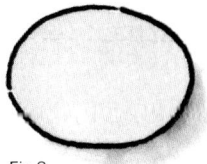

Fig 3

Fig 4

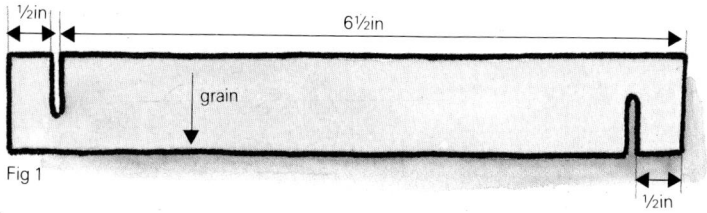

Fig 1

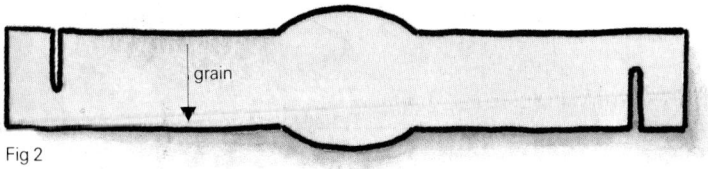

Fig 2

Below This very simple idea can be kept quite basic and unadorned or can be decorated with many of the methods already described. For example, you could attach a miniature origami butterfly, see pages 62–3, or a small paper flower, see pages 121–4. You could use a piece of marbled paper in the chosen color scheme, see pages 46–50, or write a name or initial on the ring to serve as a place name.

PLACE CARDS

EQUIPMENT

- Lightweight to mediumweight card
- Card for templates
- Paper for decorations (foil, crêpe, etc.)
- Toothpick or straw
- Glue and adhesive tape
- Pencil and ruler
- Knife or a pair of scissors

As with other items in this chapter, the place cards can be quite plain or very decorative. Folding ones, which stand up on the table, look more professional and are usually easier to read.

The names can be written with a colored pen or silver or gold markers as well as ordinary ink. The size of the card can vary a little depending on your handwriting and the length of the name, but 3–3½ in by 1¼–1½ in should allow sufficient room.

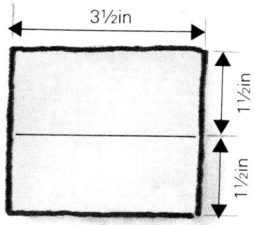

Above Here a simple place card is illustrated.

Above If one side is cut shorter than the other, the angle of the card on the table will be flatter. Draw, cut and score these cards. Then decorate them with stickers, stencil patterns, etc. Write the name on the card before folding and placing it in position.

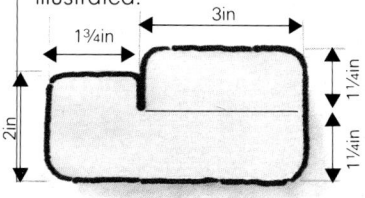

Left This place card is an adaptation of the basic card.

Below The extension could have other shapes glued to it to suit another season. It could also have quilled shapes, see pages 93–4, glued to it or a miniature origami design, see pages 58–74.

CHRISTMAS TREE DESIGN

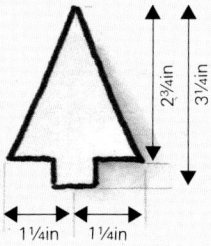

1 For a Christmas tree design you will need four of these shapes; cut them from any lightweight decorative paper. Fold each shape in half.

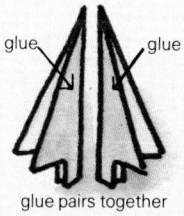

2 Glue the folded halves to each other leaving two folded halves free.

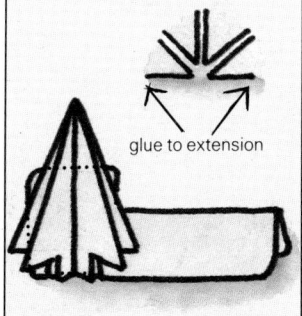

3 Glue the two free folded halves (see inset) to the side extension of the place card.

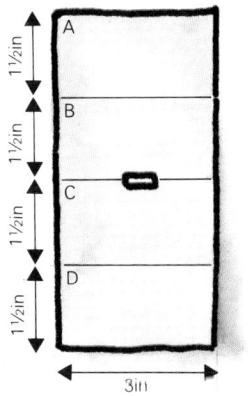

1 For the place card part of this decoration, mark a piece of card as above. Cut out the card, score and fold it and then glue section D under section A.

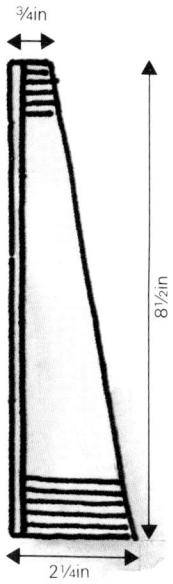

2 To make the tree use very lightweight paper. Cut out the shaped piece and attach adhesive tape along the straw. The slits should be ⅛ in apart.

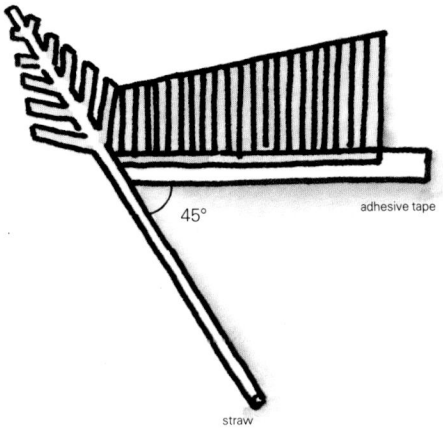

3 Take a drinking straw and, holding it at an angle of 45°, roll the adhesive tape around the straw, starting from the narrow end. The slits will fall into a tree shape. Slip the straw through the hole in the top of the card, cut it to size and then, if necessary, secure it through the base with a pin so that the tree stands upright.

Left It is possible to wrap the shaped and slit piece around the straw at an angle of 30°. This will result in a less bushy tree with a wider shape (far left). If you prefer this shape, wrap the straw with a strip of paper before winding the shaped piece around because the increased angle means that the straw will not otherwise be covered. Also the initial piece can be reduced in length by at least 2 in.
You could attach a miniature carnation, see pages 121–2, to a drinking straw or toothpick and use it in the same way. Cut leaves from suitable paper and attach them to the stem, which could be covered with stem tape or painted green.

PAPER FLOWERS

EQUIPMENT

- Stub wire (often coated with green plastic), available from florists and good craft shops
- Stem tape, also available from florists
- Crêpe paper – good-quality crêpe paper has plenty of stretch
- Pinking shears, if available.

Paper flowers are fun to make and can look quite realistic, even though they should not pretend to take the place of real flowers. As the leaves are difficult to make, it is a good idea to use real greenery in the vase; this will also help to hold the rather spindly wire stems of the paper flowers.

CARNATIONS

1 The crêpe paper should be folded to a width of 5 in. Cutting through all the thicknesses with the pinking shears, cut off the straight edge and then a piece 3½ in long. Do not unfold the paper but cut off the sides to make several rectangles with pinked edges.

2 Four layers make an average carnation, two layers make a small one and one layer makes a bud, which should be trimmed to shape on completion. Hold the layers across the width and stretch them evenly, being careful not to use your thumb tips as this will make a cupped curve at the center.

3 Turn the paper so that the short edge is facing up. Accordion pleat the length of the stretched piece – about five to six pleats ½ in wide can be fitted into the piece. It is important that the cut edges face upward at the beginning and the end. Place a stub wire in the center at the front of the pleated paper with about 1½ in showing above the folds.

4 Fold the wire down behind and twist it to secure it. Fan out the pleats to check that both sides are even.

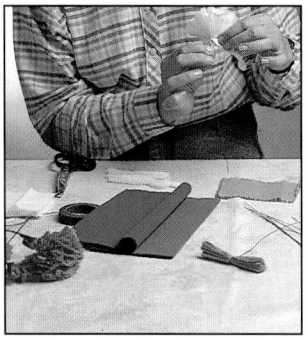

5 Now separate the layers, starting with the innermost layer, which must be pulled up as close to the wire as possible. Continue in this way until all the layers are pulled up.

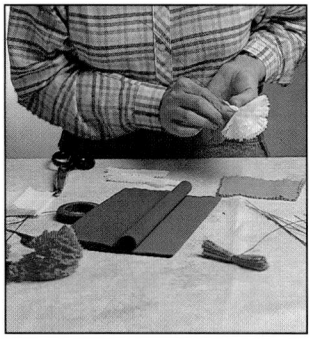

6 To make the calyx, take a piece of crêpe paper and fold it loosely into a narrow strip. Wrap it around the base of the flower, twisting the paper as it is wrapped to make it slightly triangular in shape. If you wish, use a touch of glue to secure it.

7 Take the stem tape, give it a good pull to stretch it, and then wrap it firmly around the calyx, holding the wire and pulling it downward, while twisting. It sounds complicated, but a little practice will make it clear. If stem tape is not available, a strip of green crêpe paper ½ in wide can be used and secured with glue at the top and bottom. Add leaves if you wish.

Right Make your carnations of various sizes and use different colored crêpe paper for a lovely display. If the flowers become crushed, they can be revived by holding them over steam and fluffing them up.

EQUIPMENT

- Stub wire (available as for carnations)
- Stem tape (available as for carnations)
- Florist's wire
- Double-sided crêpe paper
- Pencil
- A pair of scissors
- Blunt knife

ROSES

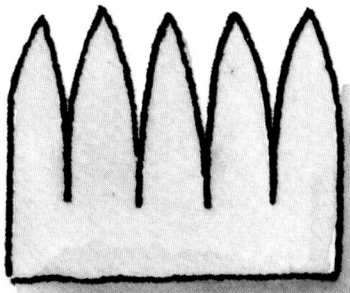

Fig 2

Above Sepal template – see step 6.

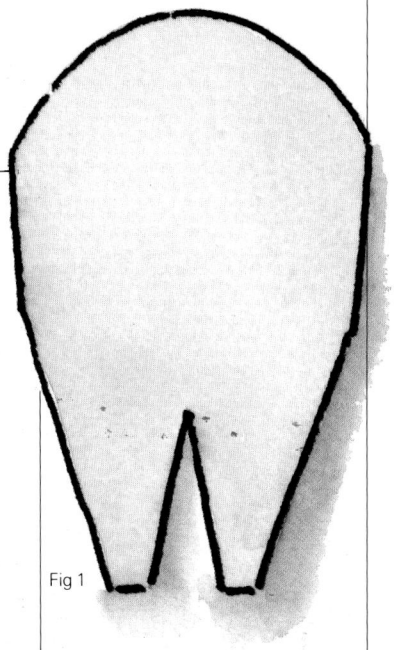

Fig 1

Right Petal template – see step 1.

1 Place the petal template (see Fig 1) on the double-sided crêpe paper and fold it over so that there are nine petals, or measure a strip approximately 18½ in and pleat it. Cut out the petal shape, making sure that the sides remain joined. Unfold and cut off three petals.

2 Decide which color should be on the outside of the petals and work with the other color facing you. Using a blunt knife or the back of the scissors, curl the petal tops by placing the blade behind the petal and gently but firmly drawing the crêpe paper over the blade.

3 Having curled all the petal tops, cup them in the center by stretching each petal across the width with your thumbs.

4 Take a stub wire and thread it through the petals at one end and turn it over to secure.

5 Now roll the first petal tightly around the wire. Ease the remaining five petals gently into shape – closed or open – and secure them by wrapping them with florist's wire. Twist the ends and bend them down.

6 Take the three separated petals and arrange them around the outside and secure them as before. The final three petals can be omitted to give a smaller rose, and if the petals are formed more tightly the result will be more bud-like. Prepare the calyx as for the carnation. Add sepals if you wish (see Fig 2) and wrap the stem as for the carnation.

Right Again, use various colors of crêpe paper for a truly marvelous and realistic bouquet of flowers.

HISTORY OF PAPER

The dictionary definition of paper is a substance made from cellulose fibers derived from rags, wood or straw often with other additives, and formed into thin, flat sheets. The word is derived from the Latin word papyrus, meaning a reed.

More than 5,000 years ago the Egyptians used these reeds, cross-woven into a mat and pounded into thin, hard sheets. However, it was a Chinese man named Ts'ai Lun, who, in A.D. 105, invented paper as we know it today.

There is evidence of papermaking in Japan around A.D. 610. The Japanese used mulberry bark and developed cottage industries in papermaking which continue to this day. Some very fine and specialized papers are made in Japan.

In A.D. 751 the Arabs captured some Chinese prisoners at Samarkand and forced them to teach them the papermaking process. The paper the Arabs produced consequently was made with linen rags. It is known that there was a papermaking factory in Baghdad in A.D. 793 with Chinese workmen. From this time onward the craft spread westwards, and when the Moors invaded Spain they introduced papermaking on a larger scale.

The earliest reference to an English paper mill is in a book printed by William Caxton, the first English printer, in about 1490. The mill belonged to John Tate of Hertfordshire and the paper was used for an edition of Chaucer's *Canterbury Tales*. Several more mills were recorded over the next 100 years but were not very successful; one reason that has been suggested is that papermakers were thought to help spread the plague by using discarded rags infected with disease.

The first known American paper mill was established at Germantown, Pennsylvania, in 1690. It used the European rag method. However, rags were becoming increasingly scarce and with the Industrial Revolution this problem became worse. As paper was still handmade, output was low, but there was an increasing demand for paper – books for the educated classes and for the poorer classes, who were beginning to be educated by charitable bodies and the Church; account books for the growing export trade; and daily newspapers were introduced at the beginning of the 18th century.

Seeing a need for machinery, Louis Robert, a clerk in a French mill, invented a crude papermaking machine in 1799. This particular machine was not very successful, but was used as the basis for an improved machine. This venture was funded by brothers Henry and Sealy Fourdrinier and developed by an engineer, Bryan Donkin. After many trials and much expense the machine was finished in 1803 and erected at Frogmore in Hertfordshire. Due to the great cost involved in developing this machine, the brothers lost a fortune, but the name of Fourdrinier lives on in the basic principles still in use today.

Paper mills today use wood pulp or recycled paper. Wood pulp comes from lumber waste and from trees, which are being constantly replaced, often by fast-growing conifers. One averaged-sized tree is needed to make sufficient paper for 400 copies of a 40-page tabloid newspaper. Newspapers are recycled into heavy-duty papers such as cardboard. There are four methods of extracting wood pulp: chemical, mechanical, semi-chemical and thermo-mechanical. Combinations of these pulps are sometimes used, depending on the use of the finished product.

Modern paper mills are extremely efficient users of energy. At one time paper mills were a major source of water pollution, but modern recycling and purification techniques have virtually eliminated this problem. Millions of gallons of water are used daily in paper manufacture – 34 percent for processing and 66 percent for cooling. All the cooling water is recycled and the processing water is purified and either discharged or re-used.

Some papers are still made by hand today, but the craft is not widely practiced; the papers that are produced are specialist papers and costly. The mechanical papermaking industry continues worldwide and is constantly improving its techniques.

INDEX

B

bags, 76, 84–6, *84–6*
  basic, 84, *84*
  bottle, 85, *85*
  equipment, 76
  heart-shaped, 86, *86*
  strong, 85
blending, 17, *17, 19*
board, 8, 9
bottle bags, 85, *85*
bowls, 17, *17*
bows, 91, *91*
boxes, 76–8, *79–83*, 80–3
  basic, 77
  collapsible, 77
  covering, 80, *80*
  equipment, 76
  flat, 81, *81*
  gift, 81
  hexagonal, 83, *83*
  pyramid, 82, *82*
  two-piece, 78, *78–9*
buckram, 112
butterfly origami, *62–3*

C

capillary matting, 17, *17*
card, 8, 9, *10*
card folds, 104, *104–5*
carnations, 121–2
Caxton, William, 125
chatterbox origami, *64–5*
Christmas decorations, *119*
coated papers, *10*, 16
collage, 34, *34*
  equipment, 34
collapsible boxes, 77
colored papers, *10, 12, 36*, 37
combing, *50*
  see also marbling
corrugated paper, 80
cotton rags, 16
couching, 22, *22–3*
covered boxes, 80, *80*
crêpe paper, *8*
cut-aways, 81, 100, *100*
  see also three-dimensional designs

D

deckle edges, 8
deckle-only method, 26, *26*
  see also mold-and-deckle method
decoration, 31–50
  boxes, *79*
  collage, 34, *34*
  dipping and folding, 42–5, *42–4*
  laid-on, 28, *28*
  marbling, 46–50
  papier mâché, *54–6*
  paste and paint, *40*
  pleating, 45
  resist methods, 38–9, *38–41*, 41
  shaped pulps, 29, *29*
  speckled sheets, 27, *27*
  stenciling, 35, *35–7*, 37
  stippling, *36*
  wax mediums, 38–9, *38–9*, 41, *41*
  weaving, 32, *32–3*
dipping and folding, 42–5, *42–4*
  equipment, 42
  see also pleating
Donkin, Bryan, 125
drying, 25, *25*

E

embossed papers, *10*
envelopes, 106, *106–8*
  basic, *106*
  folded, *107–8*
equipment, *14*
  boxes, 76
  collage, 34
  dipping, 42
  flowers, 121, 123
  marbling, 46, 47
  napkin rings, 118
  papermaking, 17, *17, 18*
  papier mâché, 52
  place cards, 119
  quills, 93
  stationery holders, 109
  stenciling, 35
  twist-outs, 96
  wax rubbings, 38
  weaving, 32

F

fish mobile, *70–1*
fish origami, *68–9*
flame napkin folds, *117*
flat boxes, 81, *81*
flowers *see* paper flowers
foil papers, *10, 36*
folded envelopes, *107–8*
folding *see* dipping and folding origami
forming paper, 20–1
Fourdrinier Brothers, 125

G

gift boxes, 81, *81*
gift tags, 92, *92*
gift-wrapping, *8, 11*
  see also bags
    boxes
    wrapping
grains, 8, 9, *9*
greeting cards, *30*, 98, *98*, 104, *104–5*

H

handles, *84, 112*
handmade paper, 8, *13*, 16, *125*
  uses of, 30
heart-shaped bags, 86, *86*
hemp, 16
hexagonal boxes, 83, *83*
history of paper, 125

I

Ingres papers, *11*, 16, 58, 88

J

Jackson, Paul, 58
Japanese box origami, *72–3*
Japanese paper, 8, *12*, 34, *54*

L

laid paper, 8
laid-on effects, 28, *28*
lens tissue, 42
lining, *113–14*

M

machinemade paper, 8, 9
making paper *see* papermaking
marbling, *13*, 46–7, *48–50*
  baths, 47
  combing, *50*
  equipment, 46, 47
  printed, 46
mobiles, 70, *70–1*
mold-and-deckle method, 17–25, *20–1*
  couching, 22, *22–3*
  drying, 25, *25*
  equipment, 17, *17*, 18
  pressing, 24, *24*
  pulp, 19, *19–21*
  see also deckle-only method
    mold-only method
moldmade paper, 8
mold-only method, 26, *26*
  see also mold-and-deckle method
molds, 8, 9, 18, *18*
multi pop-ups, 102, *102*
My Lady bow, 81, *81*

N

napkin folds, 116, *116–17*
  flames, 117
  sails, 116
napkin rings, 118, *118*
  equipment, 118
newspaper, 16, 17

O

origami, 58–9, *60–9*, 70, *70–4*
  butterfly, *62–3*
  chatterbox, *64–5*
  derivation of, 58
  fish, *68–9*
  folding, 59
  Japanese box, 72–3
  mobiles, 70, *70–1*
  paper, 58
  printer's hat, *60–1*
  repeat pattern, *66–7*
  symbols, 59, *59*
  Valentine heart, *74*
ox-gall, 46, 47
  see also marbling

P

paper, *8*
  coated, *10*, 16
  colored, *10, 12, 36*, 37
  corrugated, 80
  crêpe, *8*
  definition of, 125
  embossed, *10*
  foil, *10, 36*
  grain, 8, 9, *9*
  handmade, 8, *13*, 16, 125
  history, 125
  Ingres (Strathmore), *11*, 16, 58, 88
  Japanese, 8, *12*, 34, *54*
  laid, 8
  machinemade, 8, 9
  marbled, *13*, 46–7, *48–50*
  moldmade, 8
  origami, 58
  papier mâché, 52, *52–6*
  printed, 46
  pulp, 16
  recycled, 16
  sized, 8, 26
  strength, 8, 9, *9, 12*
  textured, *8*
  tissue, 8, *8*, 32, 34, 45, *45*, 88
  types, 16
  unsized, 8
  weight, 8
  wove, 8
  writing, 30
  see also papermaking
paper bags *see* bags
paper decoration *see* decoration
paper flowers, 121, *121–4*
  equipment, 121, 123
paper mills, 125
paper presses, 24
papermaking, 8, 15–30
  creative effects, 27–9
  deckle-only method, 26, *26*
  equipment, 17, *17, 18*
  forming, 20–1

history, 16, 125
laid-on effects, *28*
mold-and-deckle method, 17–25, *20–1*
mold-only method, 26, *26*
shaped pulps, *29*
speckled sheets, 27
suitable papers, 16
papier mâché, 52, *52–6*
decoration, *54–6*
equipment, 52
paste and paint method, *40*
place cards, 119, *119–20*
equipment, 119
plant fibers, 16
pleated wraps, *89–90*
pleating, 45
see also dipping and folding origami
pockets, 113, *113*
pop-ups, 101–2, *101–2*
multi, 102
see also three-dimensional designs
pressing, 24
printed papers, 46
printer's hat origami, *60–1*
pulp, 16, *19, 26*
wood pulp, 125
pyramid boxes, 82, *82*

Q

quills, 93–4, *94*
decoration, 94, *94*
equipment, 93
see also three-dimensional designs

R

reams, 8
recycled paper, 16
repeat pattern origami, *66–7*
resist methods, 38–9, *38–41*, 41
equipment, 38
ribbons, 91
roses, *123–4*

S

sail napkin folds, 116
sandpaper, *53*
shaped pulps, 29, *29*
sized paper, 8
sizing, 26
speckled sheets, 27, *27*
stationery, 104, *104–14*, 106, 109, 112–13
basic envelope, 106
card folds, 104, *104–5*
folded envelopes, *107–8*
holder, 109, *109–14*, 112
stationery holder, 109, *109–12*, 112
equipment, 109
lining, *113–14*
stenciling, 35, *35–7*, 37
equipment, 35
stippling, *36*
Strathmore papers *see* Ingres papers
strength, 8, 9, *9*, 12

T

table decorations, 116, *116–24*, 118–19, 121
carnations, *121–2*
flame napkin, *117*
flowers, 121, *121–4*
napkin folds, 116, *116–17*
napkin rings, 118, *118*
place cards, 119, *119–20*
roses, *123–4*
sail napkin, *116*
Tate, John, 125
textured papers, *8*
three-dimensional designs
cut-aways 81, 100, *100*
pop-ups, 101–2, *101–2*
quills, 93–4, *94*
twist-outs, 96–9, *96–9*
see also origami
ties *see* handles
tissue paper, 8, *8*, 32, 34, 42, 45, 88
Ts'ai Lun, 125
twist-outs, 96–9, *96–9*
concentric designs, 99, *99*
equipment, 96
greeting cards, 98, *98*
see also three-dimensional designs
two-piece boxes, 78, *78–9*

U

unsized paper, 8

V

Valentine heart origami, *74*

W

wallpaper paste, *40*
wastepaper baskets, 52, *56*
waterleaf paper *see* unsized paper
watermarks, 8
wax mediums, 38–9, *38–9*, 41, *41*
weaving, 32, *32–3*
equipment, 32
ribbon, 91
weight, 8
wood pulp, 125
see also pulp
wove paper, 8
wrapping, 88–9, *88–94*, 91–4
bows, 91, *91*
gift tags, 92, *92*
pleated, 89, *89–90*
quills, 93–4, *93–4*
ribbons, 91
see also bags
boxes
gift wrapping
writing paper, 30

Y

Yoshizawa, Akira, 58

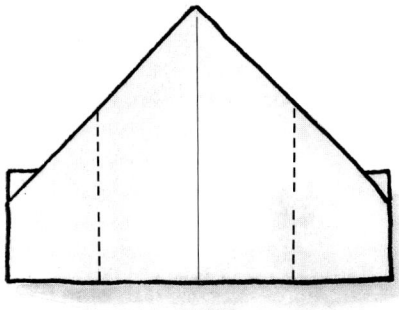